# The Competitiveness Report of Zhongguancun Listed Companies (2018)

Zhongguancun Listed Companies Association

# The Competitiveness Report of Zhongguancun Listed Companies (2018)

Springer

Zhongguancun Listed Companies
Association
Beijing, China

ISBN 978-981-13-7699-3 ISBN 978-981-13-7697-9 (eBook)
https://doi.org/10.1007/978-981-13-7697-9



This Springer imprint is published by the registered company Springer Nature Singapore Pte Ltd.
The registered company address is: 152 Beach Road, #21-01/04 Gateway East, Singapore 189721, Singapore

# Objectives

- **Observation of Authoritative Data**

Through the analysis of growth data, the study of growth pattern and the publication of the annual competitiveness report of ZLCA. This association aims to assist the government, members, and investors in their relevant project research and development strategies for member companies.

- **Communication Bridge**

We are committed in the communication between listed companies, investors, market regulators, and government in order to improve their mutual understanding by respecting needs and views.

- **Promotion for Innovation**

We strive to facilitate the development of initiative companies. We also wish to support companies listed on Growth Companies Market and promote technological innovation in Zhongguancun.

- **International Influence**

We will host international conferences, activities, and organize overseas road shows with group visits to boost the international influence of companies in Zhongguancun.

# Editorial Board of the *Competitiveness Report of Zhongguancun Listed Companies*

# Report Instruction

1. **The Competitiveness Report of Zhongguancun Listed Companies**: The Report was collected, drafted, and edited by Zhongguancun Listed Companies Association (hereinafter referred to as ZLCA), focusing on the research and study on the Zhongguancun Listed Companies (hereinafter referred to as ZLCs). "The Competitiveness Report of ZLC (2018)" refers to the report compiled based on the report of ZLC (2017) and issued in 2018.
2. **Object of Research**: Innovative high-tech companies registered in Zhongguancun National Innovation Demonstration Zone according to the *Measures on Registration Management of Zhongguancun Science and Technology Park*, listed on global capital markets, represent the new economy and lead the development of National Strategic Emerging Industries are considered as ZLCs. This report takes 312 ZLCs, with their annual reports of 2017 published before July 23, 2018, as objects of research, excluding delisted companies, firms that did not publish annual reports, businesses with their registration place changed, and other special conditions.
3. **Definitions of Key Concepts**:

   (1) **Domestic Listed Companies**: Any Zhongguancun company that listed on Shanghai Stock Exchange (hereinafter referred to as **SSE**) and Shenzhen Stock Exchange (hereinafter referred to as **SZSE**).

   (2) **Overseas Listed Companies**: Any Zhongguancun company that listed on overseas capital markets, including Hong Kong Stock Exchange (hereinafter referred to as **HKEX**), NASDAQ Stock Market (hereinafter referred to as **NASDAQ**), New York Stock Exchange (hereinafter referred to as **NYSE**), and Singapore Exchange (hereinafter referred to as **SGX**). In this report, companies listed on NASDAQ and NYSE are collectively referred to as **US listed companies** and that listed on HKEX are referred to as **HK listed companies**.

4. **Data Sources**: All financial data without special remarks was collected from the 2017 annual reports of ZLCs. The patent-related data was collected from Zhongguancun Intellectual Property Promotion Office, while the stock price

from Sina Finance (http://finance.sina.com.cn/) on the ending date of balance sheet in 2017. In addition, part of the comparative data was collected from WIND database, the database of Choice, a financial software of East Money Information, as well as the Web sites of the World Federation of Exchanges, Beijing Municipal Bureau of Statistics, SSE, SZSE, and HKEX.

5. **Methodology**: A database was created by assembling together all the public financial data of ZLCs. Based on the database, the overall competitiveness, distribution, and status of diverse industries were analyzed synchronically and diachronically. Conclusions were then drawn from the analysis, and development suggestions were proposed.
6. **Currency Unit**: RMB was used as the currency unit throughout this report. For companies listed on overseas capital markets, all the financial data was exchanged into RMB using the exchange rate of Bank of China on the ending date of balance sheet in the 2017 annual report.
7. **Data Check**: The financial data quoted in this report was collected and checked by the project team with valuable guidance and assistance from Ernst and Young Hua Ming LLP.

# About This Book

In 2017, there were 312 ZLCs distributing in major global capital markets, including 25 new listed companies which consisted of 20 domestic listed and 5 overseas listed companies. The total market capitalization of ZLCs reached 5458.9 billion yuan, a y-o-y increase of 14.7%, returning to growth after the first decline in 2016 which was influenced by the overall environment of the capital market. Among the ZLCs, Baidu, Jingdong, BOE, China Communications Construction, China Railway, and Weibo have a market capitalization of over 100 billion yuan.

From the perspective of profitability, in 2017, the total revenue of ZLCs reached 398.86 billion yuan, a y-o-y increment of 14%; the gross profit reached 803.5 billion yuan, increasing by 19% y-o-y; the total net profit was 167.8 billion, up 14% y-o-y. Among them, 263 companies achieved profitability, accounting for 84% of the total number of ZLCs, and their net profit reached 206.6 billion yuan.

From the perspective of financing, in 2017, through various financing channels, including equity financing and bond financing, ZLCs achieved a net financing amount of 226.3 billion yuan, a y-o-y decrease of 8%. The 25 new listed companies had a financing of 13.1 billion yuan for the initial public offering; Zhongguancun A-shares carried out 39 private placements, raising funds of 39.8 billion yuan; Zhongguancun Park listed companies issued 30 exchange-traded corporate bonds and raised funds of 29.2 billion yuan.

From the perspective of investment, in 2017, ZLCs achieved a net investment of 457.3 billion yuan, a y-o-y increase of 12%. In addition, the total cash and cash equivalents of ZLCs reached 874.6 billion yuan, registering a y-o-y increment of 6%. There were 14 ZLCs holding more than 10 billion yuan in cash and cash equivalents. The group of ZLCs currently has a large amount of cash available for investment.

From the perspective of R&D investment, statistics from 281 ZLCs that disclosed R&D expenses show that the R&D investment in 2017 totaled 122 billion yuan, with an average R&D intensity of 3.31%, which was higher than that of A-shares (1.5%). Among them, 151 companies had a higher R&D intensity of over 5%, while 78 of them, with a R&D intensity of more than 10%, had reached the level of international high-tech leading companies.

From the perspective of industry, information technology, industrials, consumer discretionary, and health care compose the key industries in Zhongguancun. According to the OECD classification standard, 41 ZLCs fall into the category of Internet companies (accounting for 13%) with a total market cap of 1608.4 billion yuan (accounting for 29%). Moreover, three of the six ZLCs whose market cap exceeded 100 billion yuan are Internet companies.

From the perspective of valuation, the three overall valuation indexes of domestic ZLCs in 2017 were lower than that of the previous year, which was mainly caused by the downward pressure of the domestic economy and low market sentiment. In comparison, that of overseas ZLCs increased by a certain extent compared with the previous year.

With new listed companies and delisted companies being excluded, the total market cap of the 281 consecutive trading companies rose from 4741.5 billion yuan in 2016 to 5207.6 billion yuan, registering an increase of 9.8%. The total revenue increased from 3468.8 billion yuan in 2016 to 3937.2 billion yuan, achieving a growth rate of 13.5%. The gross profit grew from 672.7 billion yuan in 2016 to 784.9 billion yuan, marking a growth rate of 16.7%. And net profit rose from 147 billion yuan in 2016 to 164.3 billion yuan, registering an increase of 11.8%. Overall, ZLCs maintained rapid growth in terms of all indicators.

In conclusion, ZLCs are distributed in major Chinese and overseas capital markets and achieved a market cap of nearly 5.5 trillion yuan. For many years, there have been leading companies with a market cap of more than 100 billion yuan. ZLCs have a complete industrial structure, covering all the national strategic emerging industries, and develop with high growth. Zhongguancun sector continues to grow steadily and develops the strength to promote strategic emerging industries. It is able to provide a major engine for future economic growth and make a greater contribution to the economic development of Zhongguancun Science Park, Beijing, and even the whole country!

# Contents

# About the Author

**Zhongguancun Listed Companies Association (ZLCA)** founded autonomously by a number of listed companies in Zhongguancun, is a national NGO registered under the Bureau of Civil Affairs of Beijing. The association was officially established on August 16, 2012.

ZLCA's mission is to assist government in delivering and implementing policies, representing members in providing advices and suggestions to government, providing professional policy consultation for its members, and establishing a high-level networking, resource sharing, and learning platform.

The foundation of ZLCA will play an important role in helping listed companies operate normatively and develop healthily, building a bridge between listed companies, investors, capital market supervisory bodies, and government, and promoting sharing of resources and cooperation.

# Chapter 1
# Overview of Zhongguancun Listed Companies in 2017

## 1.1 Distribution of Capital Markets

### *1.1.1 Overall Distribution of ZLCs in Capital Markets*

Statistics from the Administrative Committee of Z-Park show that by December 31, 2017, the number of ZLCs have grown to 320, up from 302 in 2016, registering an increase of 6%. With delisted companies, firms that did not publish annual reports and businesses with other special conditions being excluded, this report analyses 312 companies that have issued their annual reports before July 23, 2018.

ZLCs in 2017, dominated by domestic listed companies, distributed in major global capital markets. Among them, 220 are domestic listed companies, with 68 listed on the SSE and 152 on the SZSE; while 92 are overseas listed companies, including 16 on the NYSE, 24 on NASDAQ, and 52 on the HKEX (see Fig. 1.1).

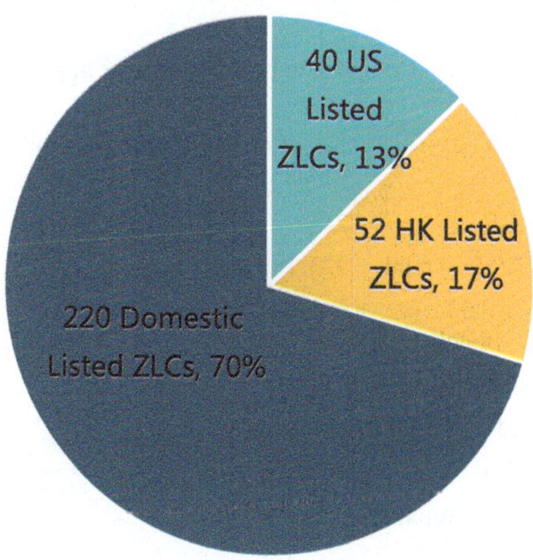


**Fig. 1.1** Distribution of ZLCs in capital markets



Zhongguancun Listed Companies Association, *The Competitiveness Report of Zhongguancun Listed Companies (2018)*,
https://doi.org/10.1007/978-981-13-7697-9_1

### 1.1.2 Distribution of New ZLCs in Capital Markets

In 2017, new listed companies in Zhongguancun increased from 20 in 2016 to 25, achieving an increment of 25%. Among them, 20 companies were listed on domestic capital markets, four in the United States and one in Hong Kong (see Fig. 1.2).

(1) Domestic Capital Markets
In 2017, the number of new listed A-shares all over China grew from 227 to 438, achieving an increase of 93% and reaching a new high. Specifically, there were 20 new listed A-shares in Zhongguancun, an increase of 42.85% compared with that in 2016 (14 in total), accounting for 4.58% of that in China (see Table 1.1).
(2) The US Capital Markets
In 2017, 220 new listed companies had been added on the US stock markets, 89 on the NASDAQ and 131 on the NYSE, seeing an increase of 50% compared with that in 2016. Among them, 26 are Chinese companies, among which four come from Zhongguancun, accounting for 1.82% of the new listed companies

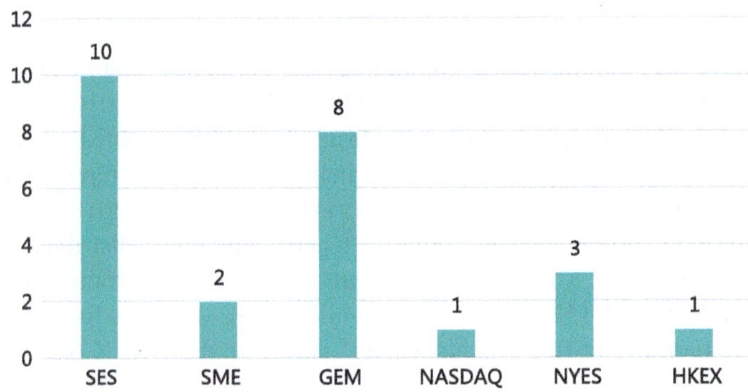


**Fig. 1.2** Distribution of new ZLCs in capital markets

**Table 1.1** Comparison between number of new listed companies in domestic capital markets and new ZLCs

| Capital markets | No. of new listed A-shares in China | No. of new listed A-shares in Zhongguancun | Percentage |
|---|---|---|---|
| SSE | 215 | 10 | 4.65 |
| SZSE in total | 223 | 10 | 4.48 |
| – Main Board | 1 | 0 | 0.00 |
| – SME | 81 | 2 | 2.47 |
| – GEM | 141 | 8 | 5.67 |
| Total | 438 | 20 | 4.57 |

*Source* WIND

**Table 1.2** Comparison between number of new listed companies on the US capital markets and new ZLCs

| Capital markets | No. of new listed companies in the US | No. of Chinese new listed companies in the US | No. of new listed ZLCs | No. of new ZLCs/No. of new listed companies in the US (%) | No. of new ZLCs/No. of new listed China concepts stocks in the US (%) |
|---|---|---|---|---|---|
| NASDAQ | 89 | 17 | 1 | 1.12 | 5.88 |
| NYSE | 131 | 9 | 3 | 2.29 | 33.33 |
| Total | 220 | 26 | 4 | 1.82 | 15.38 |

*Source* WIND, Official Website of The World Federation of Exchanges

**Table 1.3** Comparison between number of new listed companies on the HKEX and new ZLCs

| Capital markets | No. of new listed companies on HKEX | No. of new listed H-shares | No. of new ZLCs | No. of new ZLCs/No. of new listed companies on HKEX (%) | No. of new ZLCs/No. of new listed H-shares (%) |
|---|---|---|---|---|---|
| Main Board | 94 | 11 | 1 | 1.06 | 9.09 |
| Growth Enterprise Market | 80 | 2 | 0 | 0 | 0 |
| Total | 174 | 13 | 1 | 0.57 | 7.69 |

*Source* HKEX Fact Book 2017, WIND

on the US stock markets and 15.38% of new listed China Concepts Stocks (see Table 1.2).

(3) Hong Kong Capital Markets
In 2017, 174 companies were newly listed on the HKEX, including 94 on the Main Board and 80 on the Growth Enterprise Market (GEM), increasing by 38% compared with the number of new listed companies in 2016 (which totalled 126). In addition, 13 new listed H-shares landed on the HKEX, including 11 on the Main Board and 2 on the GEM. In 2017, only one Zhongguancun company was newly listed on the Hong Kong Main Board, a decrease of 66.67% compared with that in 2016 (3 in total), accounting for 0.01% of the new listed companies on the HKEX and 7.69% of the new listed H-shares (see Table 1.3).

Overall, compared with 2016, the number of new listed companies in the global capital markets had seen a sharp rise in 2017, especially in the A-share market. In 2017, the number of new listed A-shares exceeded 400 for the first time and the number of new IPOs reached 438, exceeding the historical high of 348 in 2010. The reason for the sharp increase in the number of new listed companies on the Shanghai and Shenzhen stock markets lied in the gradually accelerated IPO review in the first three quarters of 2017. According to statistics from WIND, from January to the end of September 2017, the national average pass rate was 80.99%, while Beijing had a pass rate of 82.61% and Zhongguancun 84.21%. Since October 2017, the new Issuance Appraisal Committee has adopted a stricter review standard for companies. They not only review financial indicators, but also take non-financial indicators into account, ranging from corporate governance norms, information disclosure compliance, development prospects to corporate sustainable profitability, resulting in a slowdown in the increase of new listed companies. From October 2017 to the end of July 2018, the national average pass rate dropped to 51.44%, while that of Beijing decreased to 44.00% and Zhongguancun 38.10%.

New ZLCs on the domestic stock markets have seen a slower increase rate and a lower pass rate in recent years. The main reason is that the pre-IPOs in Zhongguancun are dominated by technology-based companies. These companies are characterized by high investment in the early stage of research and development, slow profitability and great uncertainty, making it difficult to meet the requirements of continuous profit and net operate loss in the current listing and issuance standards in mainland China. Moreover, many of these enterprises, engaging in frontier fields like the Internet, big data, artificial intelligence and life sciences, possess new technologies and new models which are pioneering in China and different from the features and development models of traditional companies. This, to some extent, compounds the difficulty of the review on listing.

## 1.2 Distribution of Industries

In view of the fact that ZLCs are distributed in the world's major capital markets, this report adopts two industry classification standards: the WIND industry classification that meets international standards and the OECD's classification for Internet and non-Internet companies.

The most distinctive feature of the WIND industry classification standard lies in the comprehensive reference to the canonical GICS[1] (Global Industry Classification Standard). Combining the GICS four-tier industry system with China's actual situation, WIND established the industry classification standard that meets both international standards and the conditions of the Chinese market. It consists of 11 primary industry indicators (including Energy, Materials, Industrials, Consumer Discretionary, Consumer Staples, Health Care, Financials, Information Technology, Telecommunication Services, Utilities and Real Estate), 24 secondary, 69 tertiary and 161 quaternary industry indicators. This report divides the 312 ZLCs into diverse industries according to WIND's four-tier industry indicators.

[1]GICS is an industry taxonomy developed by MSCI and S&P and most extensively used in the global financial community.

OECD (Organization for Economic Co-operation and Development) divides Internet companies into three categories[2]: Basic and Search Engine Services, Internet Security and Software Services, and Internet Intermediaries. This report classifies the 312 ZLCs into Internet and Non-Internet companies in terms of the OECD standard.

### *1.2.1 Classification in Terms of the WIND Standard*

According to the classification results, "Information Technology" represented by Internet Software and Services, Information Technology Services, Software and other industries, "Industrials" represented by Electrical Equipment, Construction and Engineering, Commercial Services and Supplies, Aerospace and Defense, "Consumer Discretionary" represented by Media and Comprehensive Consumer Services, and "Health Care" represented by Biotechnology, Medical Care Equipment and Supplies, and Pharmaceuticals compose the key industries among ZLCs. Meanwhile, there are also companies engaged in such industries as "Materials", "Energy" and "Utilities" (see Table 1.4).

### *1.2.2 Internet and Non-internet Companies in Zhongguancun*

Few ZLCs fall into the category of Internet companies and most of them are US listed companies. According to the OECD's standards of Internet companies and non-Internet companies, there are 41 Internet companies, accounting for 13%, and 271 non-Internet companies among ZLCs, accounting for 87%. From the perspective of stock markets where companies got listed, there are 15 Internet companies (accounting for 7%) and 205 non-Internet companies (accounting for 93%) in the 220 domestic listed companies; five of the 52 HK listed companies are Internet companies (accounting for 10%) and 47 non-Internet companies (accounting for 90%); while 21 of the 40 US listed companies are Internet companies (accounting for 53%) and 19 non-Internet companies (accounting for 47%) (see Fig. 1.3).

A conclusion can be drawn from the above data: compared with the strict review and approval system in mainland China, the relatively lenient listing requirements have attracted a large number of Internet companies to get listed in the US. However, since the second half of 2017, the concept of the new economy has grown into a hit in the Hong Kong capital markets, hence the trend of listing in Hong Kong for new economy companies. Moreover, the "weighted voting rights" reform launched by the HKSE in 2018 further promoted the enthusiasm for the Internet, technology

[2]Source: OECD (2010), OECD Information Technology Outlook 2010, OECD Publishing, Paris. http://dx.doi.org/10.1787/it_outlook-2010-en.

**Table 1.4** Classification of ZLCs in terms of the WIND Standard

| Primary industries | No. | Secondary industries | No. | Tertiary industries | No. | Quaternary industries | No. |
|---|---|---|---|---|---|---|---|
| Information Technology | 127 | Software & Services | 90 | Internet Software & Services III | 28 | Internet Software & Services | 28 |
| | | | | IT Service | 29 | IT Consulting and Other Services | 25 |
| | | | | | | Data Processing & Outsourcing Services | 4 |
| | | | | Software | 33 | Application Software | 25 |
| | | | | | | System Software | 3 |
| | | | | | | Home Entertainment Software | 5 |
| | | Technical Hardware and Equipment | 31 | Communications Equipment III | 9 | Communications Equipment | 9 |
| | | | | Computers & Peripherals | 5 | Computer Hardware | 3 |
| | | | | | | Computer Storage & Peripherals | 2 |
| | | | | Electronic Equipment, Instruments & Components | 17 | Electronic Components | 3 |
| | | | | | | Electronic Equipment and Instruments | 11 |
| | | | | | | Technical Product Distributor | 3 |
| | | Semiconductors & Semiconductor Equipment II | 6 | Semiconductors & Semiconductor Equipment III | 6 | Semiconductors | 5 |
| | | | | | | Semiconductor Equipment | 1 |

(continued)

**Table 1.4** (continued)

| Primary industries | No. | Secondary industries | No. | Tertiary industries | No. | Quaternary industries | No. |
|---|---|---|---|---|---|---|---|
| Industrials | 73 | Capital Goods | 57 | Aerospace & Defense III | 9 | Aerospace & Defense | 9 |
| | | | | Building ProductsIII | 6 | Building Products | 6 |
| | | | | Construction & Engineering III | 14 | Construction & Engineering | 14 |
| | | | | Electrical Equipment | 15 | Electrical Components & Equipment | 12 |
| | | | | | | Heavy Electrical Equipment | 3 |
| | | | | Industrial Conglomerates III | 2 | Industrial Conglomerates | 2 |
| | | | | Machinery | 8 | Industrial Machinery | 7 |
| | | | | | | Construction & Farm Machinery & Heavy Trucks | 1 |
| | | | | Trading Companies & Distributors III | 3 | Trading Companies & Distributors | 3 |
| | | Commercial & Professional Services | 15 | Commercial Services & Supplies | 10 | Commercial Printing | 1 |
| | | | | | | Environmental & Facilities Services | 9 |
| | | | | Professional Service | 5 | Research & Consulting Services | 5 |
| | | Transportation | 1 | Road & Rail Transportation | 1 | Road Transportation | 1 |
| Consumer Discretionary | 41 | Automobiles & Components | 2 | Automobiles | 2 | Automobile Manufacturers | 2 |
| | | Consumer Services II | 11 | Hotels, Restaurants & Leisure III | 2 | Hotels, Resorts & Cruise Lines | 2 |
| | | | | Diversified Consumer Services | 9 | Education Services | 9 |

(continued)

**Table 1.4** (continued)

| Primary industries | No. | Secondary industries | No. | Tertiary industries | No. | Quaternary industries | No. |
|---|---|---|---|---|---|---|---|
| | | Media II | 16 | Media III | 16 | Advertising | 6 |
| | | | | | | Cable & Satellite | 2 |
| | | | | | | Broadcasting | 1 |
| | | | | | | Movies & Entertainment | 4 |
| | | | | | | Publishing | 3 |
| | | Durable Consumer Goods and Clothing | 6 | Textiles, Clothing and Luxury Goods | 6 | Clothing, Apparel and Luxury Goods | 6 |
| | | Retailing | 6 | Consumer Goods Distributors III | 1 | Consumer Goods Distributors | 1 |
| | | | | Internet & Catalog Retail | 2 | Internet Retail | 2 |
| | | | | Multiline Retail | 1 | Department Stores | 1 |
| | | | | Specialty Retail | 2 | Computer & Electronics Retail | 1 |
| | | | | | | Automotive Retail | 1 |
| Health Care | 31 | Health Care Equipment & Services | 12 | Health Care Equipment & Supplies | 8 | Health Care Supplies | 2 |
| | | | | | | Health Care Equipment | 6 |
| | | | | Health Care Providers & Services | 4 | Health Care Distributors | 2 |
| | | | | | | Health Care Facilities | 1 |
| | | | | | | Health Care Services | 1 |
| | | Pharmaceuticals, Biotechnology & Life Sciences | 19 | Biotechnology III | 10 | Biotechnology | 10 |
| | | | | Pharmaceuticals III | 8 | Western Medicine | 6 |
| | | | | | | Chinese Traditional Medicine | 2 |

(continued)

**Table 1.4** (continued)

| Primary industries | No. | Secondary industries | No. | Tertiary industries | No. | Quaternary industries | No. |
|---|---|---|---|---|---|---|---|
| | | | | Life Sciences Tools & Services III | 1 | Life Sciences Tools & Services | 1 |
| Materials | 16 | Materials II | 16 | Chemicals | 3 | Commodity Chemicals | 2 |
| | | | | | | Specialty Chemicals | 1 |
| | | | | Construction Materials III | 7 | Construction Materials | 7 |
| | | | | Containers & Packaging | 1 | Metal & Glass Containers | 1 |
| | | | | Metals, Nonmetals & Mining | 5 | Metals & Nonmetals | 5 |
| Energy | 7 | Energy II | 7 | Energy Equipment & Services | 6 | Oil & Gas Equipment & Services | 6 |
| | | | | Oil, Gas & Consumable Fuels | 1 | Coal & Consumable Fuels | 1 |
| Utilities | 6 | Utilities II | 6 | Independent Power Producers & Energy Traders III | 3 | New Energy Power Producers | 3 |
| | | | | Multi-Utilities III | 1 | Multi-Utilities | 1 |
| | | | | Water Utilities III | 1 | Water Utilities | 1 |
| | | | | Gas Utilities III | 1 | Gas Utilities | 1 |
| Consumer Staple | 5 | Food, Beverage & Tobacco | 5 | Beverages | 1 | Brewers | 1 |
| | | | | Food Products | 4 | Agricultural Products | 2 |
| | | | | | | Packaged Foods & Meats | 2 |

(continued)

**Table 1.4** (continued)

| Primary industries | No. | Secondary industries | No. | Tertiary industries | No. | Quaternary industries | No. |
|---|---|---|---|---|---|---|---|
| Financials | 2 | Diversified Financials | 2 | Diversified Financial Services | 1 | Multi-Sector Holdings | 1 |
| | | | | Consumer Credit III | 1 | Consumer Credit | 1 |
| Telecommunication Services | 2 | Telecommunication Services II | 2 | Diversified Telecommunication Services | 1 | Integrated Telecommunication Services | 1 |
| | | | | Wireless Telecommunication Services III | 1 | Wireless Telecommunication Services | 1 |
| Real Estate | 2 | Real EstateII | 2 | Real Estate Management & Development | 2 | Real Estate Development | 2 |

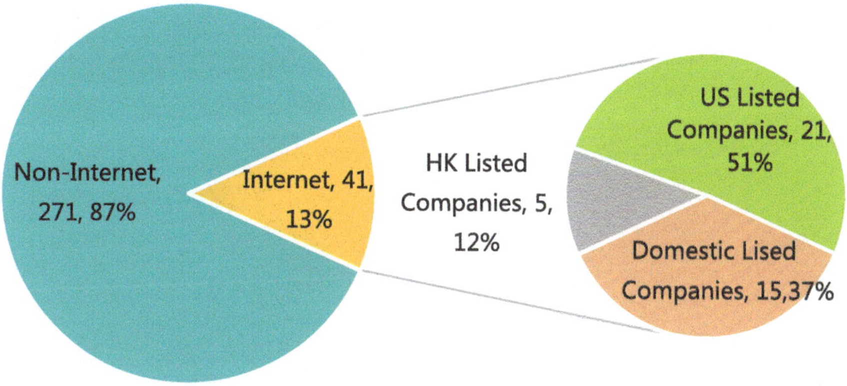


**Fig. 1.3** Internet and non-internet ZLCs in 2017

and other economic companies to list in Hong Kong. As a result, in the first half of 2018, the Hong Kong stock markets had seen increasingly many Internet companies list or file for IPO there.

# Chapter 2
# The Market Performance of ZLCs in 2017

## 2.1 Zhongguancun Stock Index

In order to better reflect the performance of ZLCs, the ZLCA and the Shenzhen Stock Exchange jointly developed the Zhongguancun Stock Index in early 2014. The index, whose compiling plan is internationally compatible, is designed to be a benchmark index that represents the level of innovation in China's science and technology sector. Though mainly including A-share listed companies for the present, the index will trace overseas listed companies in the future. The ZLCA is expected to develop more indexes related to Zhongguancun and ZLCs. The Zhongguancun Stock Index is currently made up of the Zhongguancun A-share Composite Index (Z-Park A-share Index) and the Zhongguancun 50 index (Z-Park 50 Index), which were officially released on February, 2015, and the SZSE Zhongguancun Non-SOE 60 Index (Z-Park 60 Index), which debuted on January 10, 2017. The three indexes all take December 31, 2008 as the base date and 1000 point as the base value. The Z-Park A-Share Index traces all A-share listed companies registered in the Z-Park. It is a comprehensive index reflecting the overall performance of ZLCs. The Z-Park 50 Index reflects market performance of ZLCs with large market capitalisation and good liquidity, highlighting their investment value. The Z-Park 60 Index takes Z-Park registered private enterprises which listed in Shenzhen Market as sample space, offering a scale plate for the performance of these companies.

As statistics showed, from the base date to December 31, 2017, the accumulative yields of Z-Park A-share Index, Z-Park 50 Index, and Z-Park 60 Index reached 218, 189, and 370%, respectively. Their accumulative excess return rates were 97, 68, and 249%, comparing to the CSI 300 Index in the same period, 121, 92, and 273%, comparing to the Hang Seng Index, and 35, 6, and 187%, comparing to the S&P 500 (Fig. 2.1).


Zhongguancun Listed Companies Association, *The Competitiveness Report of Zhongguancun Listed Companies (2018)*,
https://doi.org/10.1007/978-981-13-7697-9_2

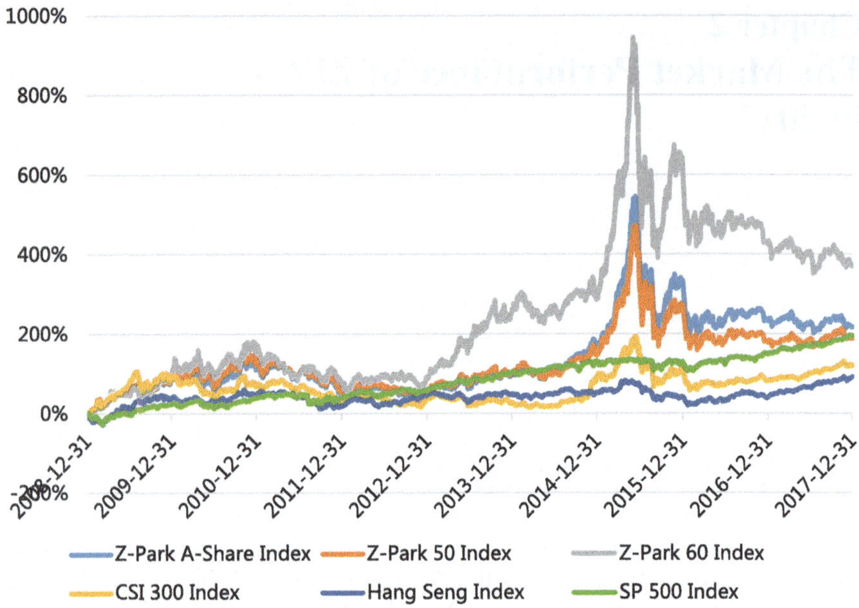


**Fig. 2.1** Accumulative return rates of Z A-share Index, Z 50 Index, Z 60 Index, CSI 300 Index, SP500 Index and Hang Seng Index from 2008/12/31 to 2017/12/31

## 2.2 Market Capitalisation of ZLCs

### *2.2.1 Total Market Capitalisation of ZLCs*

On December 31, 2017, the total market capitalisation of ZLCs reached 5458.9 billion yuan, increasing by 14.71% y-o-y, while the total market capitalisation of China's A-share listed companies[1] increased by 12.43% in 2017. The GDP of Beijing[2] in 2017 was 2800.04 billion yuan, representing a y-o-y increase of 6.7%. This shows that the total market capitalisation of ZLCs has resumed its growth after the first decline in 2016 due to the impact of the overall environment of the capital market. It is now close to twice the GDP of Beijing (see Fig. 2.2).

Domestic listed companies accounted for a major proportion of the total market capitalisation of ZLCs, followed by U.S. listed companies and Hong Kong listed companies. In terms of growth, the total market capitalisation of U.S. listed companies saw the greatest increase, followed by that of Hong Kong listed companies, while the market capitalisation of domestic listed companies declined. The market capitalisation of domestic listed companies was 3258.9 billion yuan, accounting for 60% of the total market capitalisation of ZLCs and dropping 2% y-o-y. Influenced

[1] Data source: WIND and ZLCA.

[2] Data source: Official website of Beijing Municipal Bureau of Statistics.

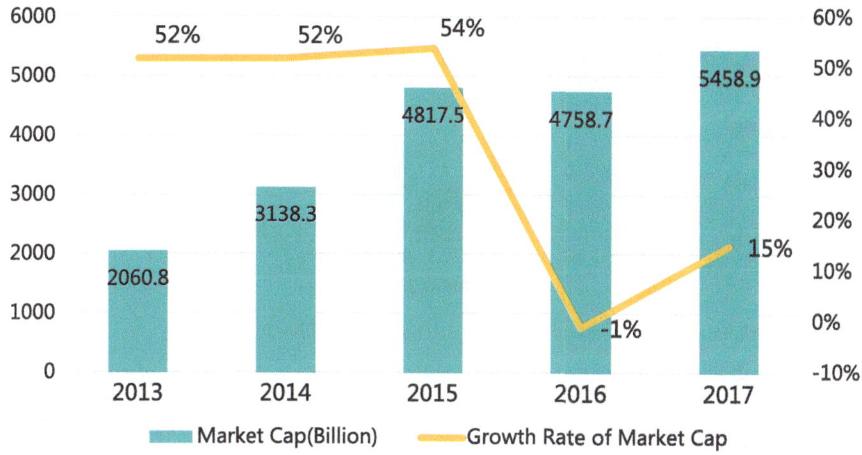


**Fig. 2.2** Market cap of ZLCs from 2013 to 2017

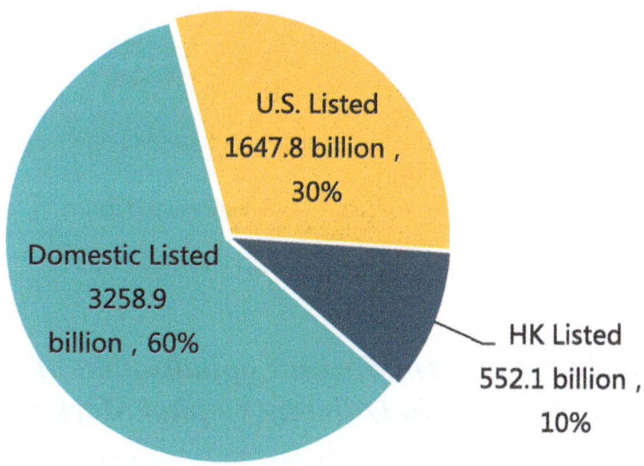


**Fig. 2.3** Proportions of market cap of ZLC in 2017

by the overall economic situation, 155 ZLCs saw decline in their market capitalisation to varying degrees. The market capitalisation of overseas listed companies was 2199.9 billion yuan, accounting for 40% of the total market capitalisation of ZLCs and increasing by 52% y-o-y. Among overseas listed companies, the total market capitalisation of U.S. listed companies was 1647.8 billion yuan, accounting for 30% of the total market capitalisation of ZLCs and increasing by 70% over the previous year (Fig. 2.3). The market capitalisation of U.S. listed companies has dramatically risen for two reasons: first, Sogou just went public on the U.S. stock market; second, the market capitalisation of Baidu, Jingdong, New Oriental and other companies rose sharply. The total market capitalisation of Hong Kong listed companies was 552.1 billion yuan, which was 10% of the total, increasing by 17% over the previous year (see Fig. 2.4).

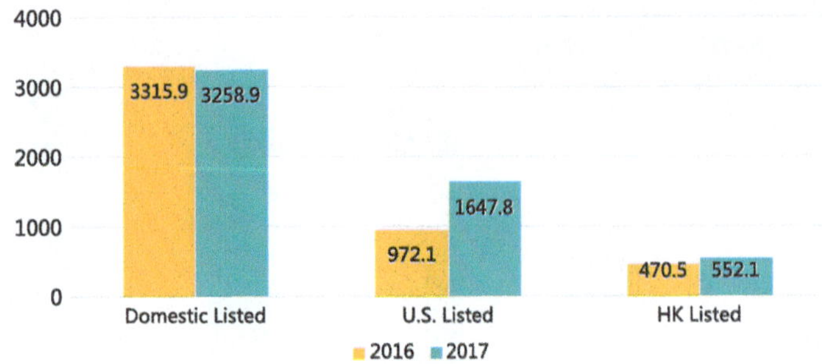


**Fig. 2.4** Market cap in each capital market in 2016–2017 (¥ billions)

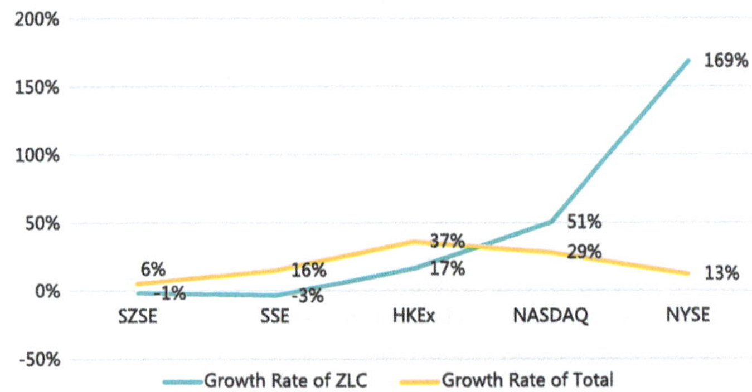


**Fig. 2.5** Market cap of ZLCs on different capital markets and total averages

### 2.2.2 *Comparison Between Market Capitalisation of ZLCs and Total Averages in Different Capital Markets*

In 2017, the market capitalisation of ZLCs on the Nasdaq and NYSE was significantly higher than the total averages, while the situation was on the opposite on the SZSE, SSE and HKEx. Specifically, the market capitalisation of Zhongguancun companies listed on the Nasdaq increased by 51%, while the total market capitalisation of Nasdaq rose only 29%; the market capitalisation of ZLCs on the NYSE rose by 169%, and the total average saw a rather small growth of 13%; the market capitalisation of ZLCs on the SZSE decreased by 1%, while the total average of SZSE rose by 6%; the market capitalisation of ZLCs on the SSE decreased by 3%, while the total average dropped 16%; the market capitalisation of ZLCs on the HKEx rose by 17%, while the total average of the HKEx rose by 37% (see Fig. 2.5).

Besides RETO ECO-SOLUTIONS, a new listed company, Jingdong, Baidu and Weibo all contributed to the large increase in the market capitalisation of ZLCs on the Nasdaq. As for the ZLCs on the NYSE, the newly listed Sogou, RYB Education and Jianpu Technology were major growth drivers, as well as New Oriental, 58.COM, and Autohome. However, 68% of ZLCs on the SSE (46 companies), 72% of ZLCs on the SZSE (109 companies) and 60% of ZLCs the HKEx (31 companies) reported decline in their market capitalisation in late 2017.

### 2.2.3 *Market Capitalisation Distribution*

In 2017, a few large ZLCs contributed a huge amount of market capitalisation. Actually, the top 20% accounted for 70% of the total. Large-scale superior companies are leading regional economic development. At the same time, the number of small and medium-sized companies with good potential and prospect is huge. More ZLCs are expected to have a market capitalisation of over 100 billion yuan.

Among the 312 ZLCs, there were six companies with a market capitalisation of over 100 billion yuan, accounting for 2% of the total; their market capitalisation reached 1632.2 billion yuan, which was 30% of the total. There were 13 companies with a market capitalisation of 50–100 billion yuan, accounting for 4% of the total; their market capitalisation was 884.3 billion yuan in addition, namely 16% of the total. There were 43 companies with a market capitalisation of 20–50 billion yuan, accounting for 14% of the total; their market capitalisation summed up to 1334.7 billion yuan, which took up 24% of the total. There were 52 companies with a market capitalisation of 10–20 billion yuan, accounting for 17% of the total, and their market capitalisation was 740.7 billion yuan, accounting for 14% of the total. There were 77 companies with a market capitalisation of 5–10 billion yuan, accounting for 25% of the total; their market capitalisation was 549.7 billion yuan, accounting for 10% of the total. There were 121 companies with a market capitalisation of less than 5 billion yuan, accounting for 39% of the total; their market capitalisation reached 317.3 billion yuan, accounting for 6% of the total (see Fig. 2.6).

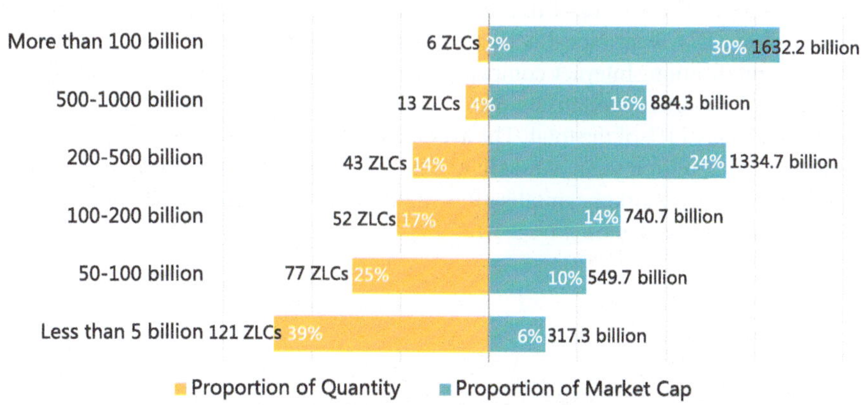


**Fig. 2.6** Distribution of market cap of ZLCs in 2017 (¥ billions)

### 2.2.4 Ranking of Market Capitalisation

At the end of 2017, the market capitalisation of the ZLCs on the top 30 ranking reached 2987.3 billion yuan, accounting for 55% of the total. The market capitalisation of the company that ranked 30th was 37.3 billion yuan. Private companies on the ranking of 2017 were Baidu, Jingdong, Weibo, New Oriental, TAL, Sany, 58.COM, SJEP, LeTV, BOW, DFYL, Autohome, Sina, Lepu Medical, Xinwei Group, CITIC GUOAN INFO. Among them, TAL, 58.COM, Autohome, Sina, Lepu Medical, BNBMPLC were newly included in 2017.

According to Wind's Primary Industry Classification standards, the top 30 ZLCs were mainly in three industries: IT (12), Industrial (6), and Consumer Discretionary (5). The rest were in Health Care (2), Materials (2), Financials (1), Utilities (1), and Telecommunications Services (1). There were seven Internet-based companies on the ranking of 2017, namely Baidu, Jingdong, Weibo, 58.COM, LeTV, Autohome, Sina, and the remaining 23 were non-Internet companies (see Fig. 2.7).

### 2.2.5 Market Capitalisation Distribution

ZLCs in IT, Industrial and Consumer Discretionary accounted for the majority of market capitalisation in 2017—2408.5 billion yuan, 1177.7 billion yuan and 986.8 billion yuan respectively. The market capitalisation of those companies equalled 84% of the total (see Fig. 2.8). In terms of the average market capitalisation of different industries, ZLCs in four industries of Financials, Telecommunications Services, Consumer Discretionary and IT were superior to the overall average (17.5 billion yuan) (see Fig. 2.9).

The number of Internet-based ZLCs was small, but their average market capitalisation was high. There were 41 Internet-based ZLCs, which took up 13% of the total; the remaining 271 were Non-Internet companies, accounting for 87%. In terms of market capitalisation, Internet companies accounted for 29%, reaching 1608.4 billion yuan; the market capitalisation of Non-Internet companies was 3850.5 billion yuan, which was 71% of the total. The average market capitalisation of Internet companies was 39.2 billion yuan, while that of Non-Internet companies was 14.2 billion yuan. The average market capitalisation of Internet companies was 2.76 times that of Non-Internet companies (Fig. 2.10).

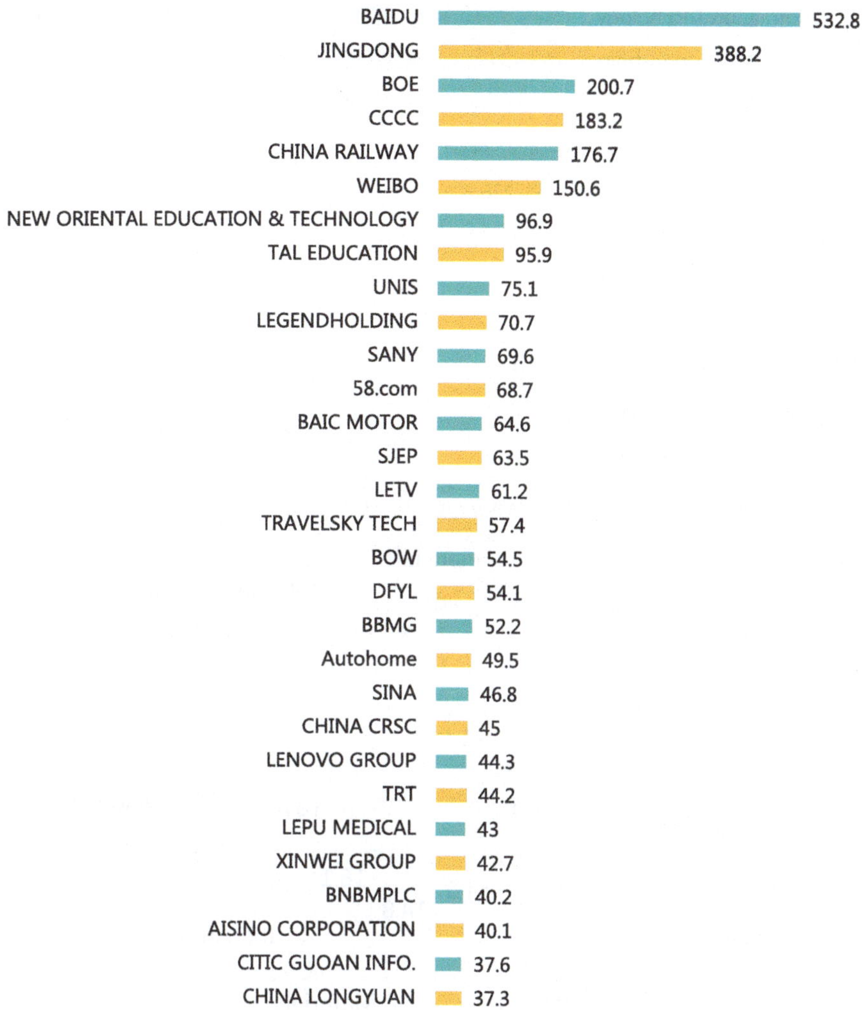


**Fig. 2.7** Market cap of the top 30 ZLCs (¥ billions)

## 2.3 Valuation of ZLCs

### *2.3.1 Overall Valuation*

In 2017, the overall P/B ratio of ZLCs was 2.35. Among them, the P/B ratio of domestic listed companies was 2.28, and that of overseas listed companies was 2.45. The P/B ratio of U.S. listed Zhongguancun companies was 4.66, and that of companies listed the Hong Kong was 1.02.

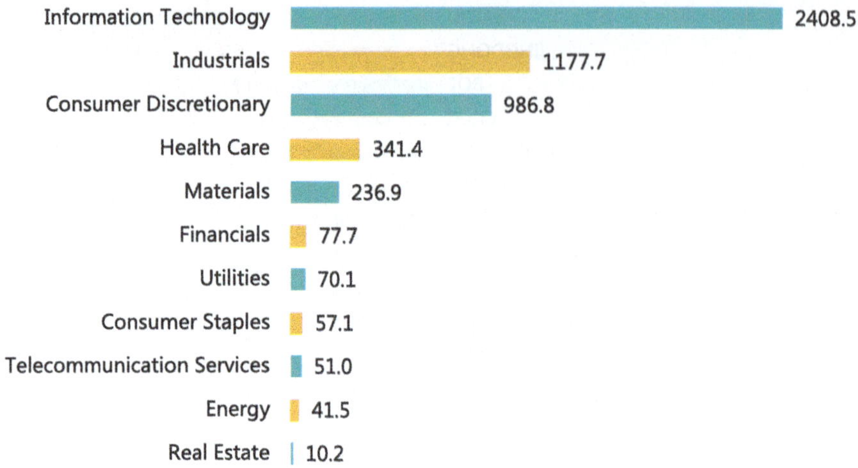


**Fig. 2.8** Market cap of ZLCs in each industry in 2017 (¥ billions)

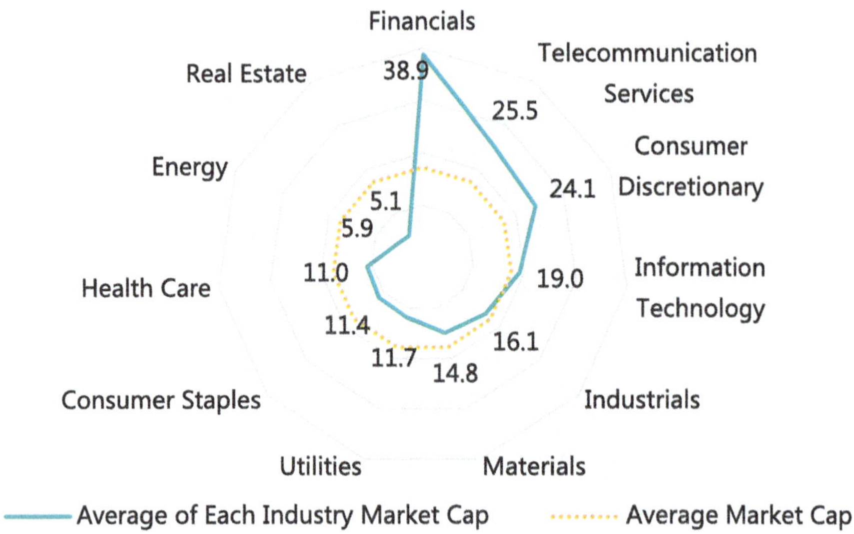


**Fig. 2.9** Average Market cap of ZLCs in each industry in 2017 (¥ billions)

In 2017, the overall P/S rate of ZLCs was 1.37. Among them, the P/S ratio of domestic listed companies was 1.49, and that of overseas listed companies was 1.22. The P/S ratio of U.S. listed Zhongguancun companies was 2.81, and that of companies listed the Hong Kong was 0.46.

In 2017, the overall P/E ratio of ZLCs was 32.53. Among them, the P/E ratio of domestic listed companies was 34.63, and that of overseas listed companies was 29.86. The P/E ratio of U.S. listed Zhongguancun companies was 66.80, and that of companies listed the Hong Kong was 11.27. With loss-making companies excluded,

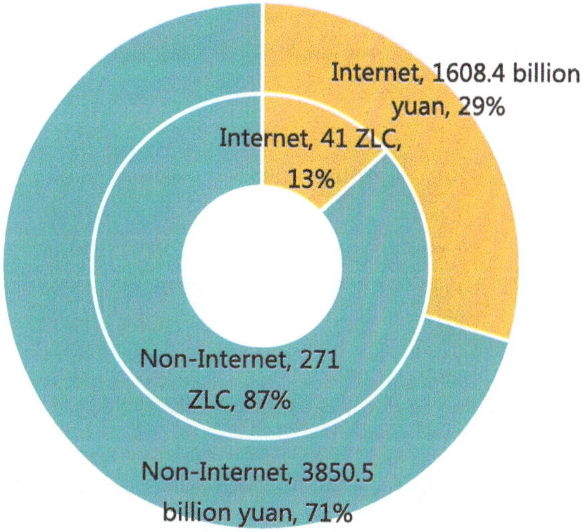


**Fig. 2.10** Distribution of Number and Market cap of Internet ZLCs and Non-Internet ZLCs in 2017

the overall P/E ratio of ZLCs in 2017 was 22.81, among which the domestic listed companies had a P/E ratio of 25.61, and the overseas listed companies had a P/E ratio of 18.97 (the P/E ratio of U.S. listed companies was 33.25, and the P/E ratio of Hong Kong listed companies was 9.25).

The three valuation indicators—P/B ratio, P/S ratio and P/E ratio—of domestic listed Zhongguancun companies declined over the previous, which is mainly contributed to downward pressure on the Chinese economy and low market sentiment. For overseas listed companies, the three indicators increased compared to the previous year mostly because long-term expectation on U.S. stocks were rising in the amidst of the second longest bull market ever recorded. Similar to 2016, the valuation of domestic listed Zhongguancun companies, except the P/B ratio, was generally higher than that of overseas listed companies. This shows that the domestic capital market will continue to play a greater role in the development of ZLCs (Table 2.1).

### 2.3.2 *Valuation of ZLCs in Different Industries*

By comparing the three valuation indicators of ZLCs in different industries, it can be concluded that key and leading companies in Information Technology had the highest valuation, for the three valuation indicators of those companies were higher than the overall average. Companies in Health care, Consumer Discretionary and Consumer Staples were only inferior to IT companies. The P/B ratio and P/S ratio of companies in Health Care exceeded the overall average; the P/B ratio and P/E ratio of companies in Consumer Discretionary were higher than the overall average; the P/S ratio and P/E

**Table 2.1** Valuation of ZLCs (2016–2017)

| Capital markets | P/B ratio[a] | | P/S ratio[b] | | P/E ratio[c] | | P/E ratio[d] (excluding loss-making companies) | |
|---|---|---|---|---|---|---|---|---|
| | 2016 | 2017 | 2016 | 2017 | 2016 | 2017 | 2016 | 2017 |
| Domestic | 2.93 | 2.28 | 1.73 | 1.49 | 35.53 | 34.63 | 31.72 | 25.61 |
| Overseas | 2.25 | 2.45 | 0.92 | 1.22 | 26.84 | 29.86 | 14.84 | 18.97 |
| – US | 3.75 | 4.66 | 2.25 | 2.81 | 101.70 | 66.80 | 29.85 | 33.25 |
| – HK | 1.24 | 1.02 | 0.42 | 0.46 | 10.65 | 11.27 | 8.52 | 9.25 |
| Overall | 2.68 | 2.35 | 1.37 | 1.37 | 32.35 | 32.53 | 24.73 | 22.81 |

[a]P/B ratio = total market cap/net asset (equity attributed to shareholders of the parent company)
[b]P/S ratio = total market cap/total income
[c]P/E ratio = total market cap/net income
[d]P/E ratio (excluding Loss-Making Companies) = total market cap of profitable companies/net income of profitable companies

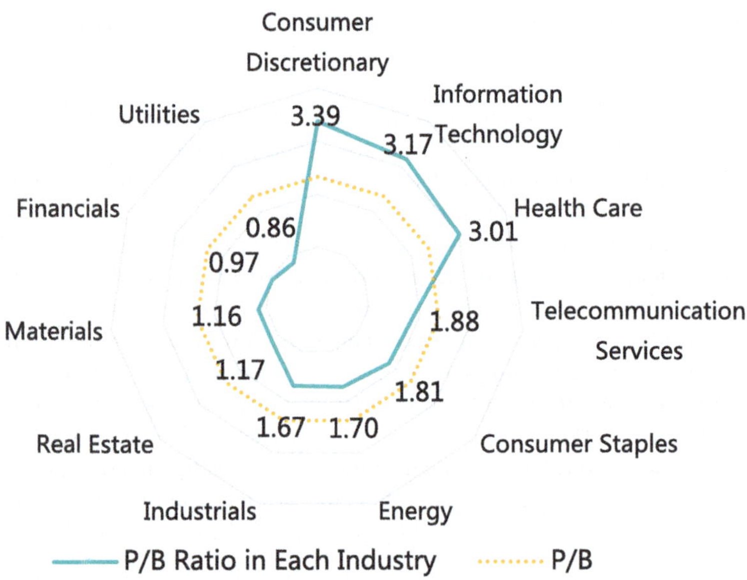


**Fig. 2.11** P/B of ZLCs in each industry in 2017

ratio of companies in Consumer Staples beat the overall average. This shows that the capital market has higher expectation these industries in Zhongguancun. However, for industries that are relatively mature such as Materials, Telecommunications Services, Industrials, Utilities, the market has relatively reasonable expectation (Figs. 2.11, 2.12, 2.13 and 2.14).

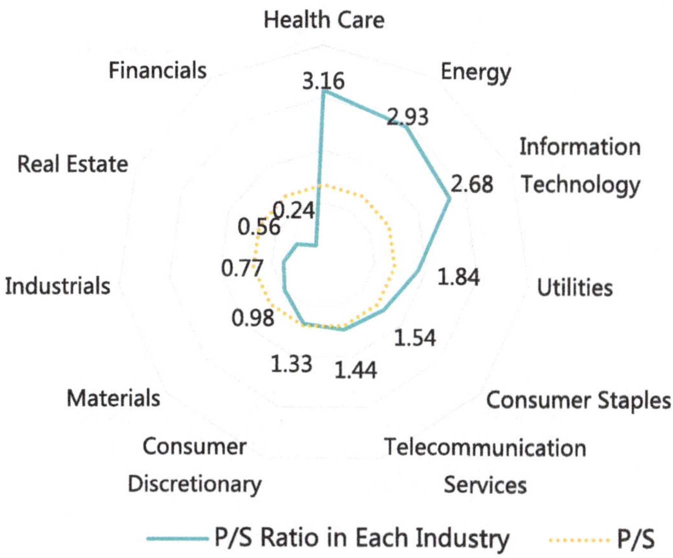


**Fig. 2.12** P/S of ZLCs in each industry in 2017

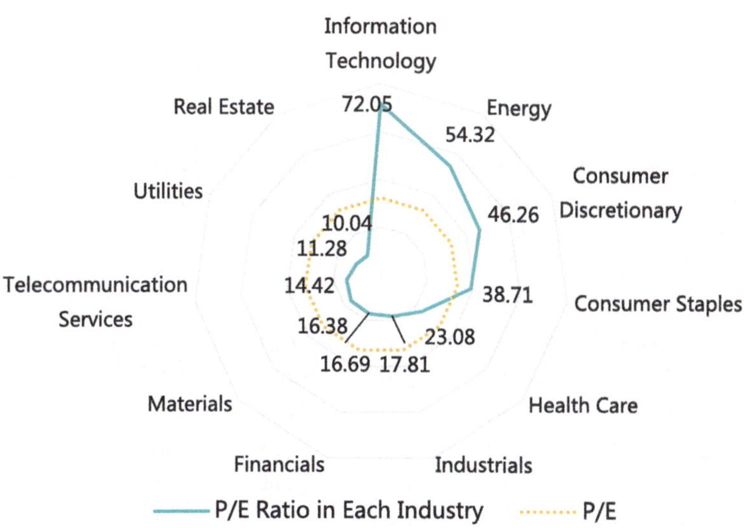


**Fig. 2.13** P/E of ZLCs in each industry in 2017

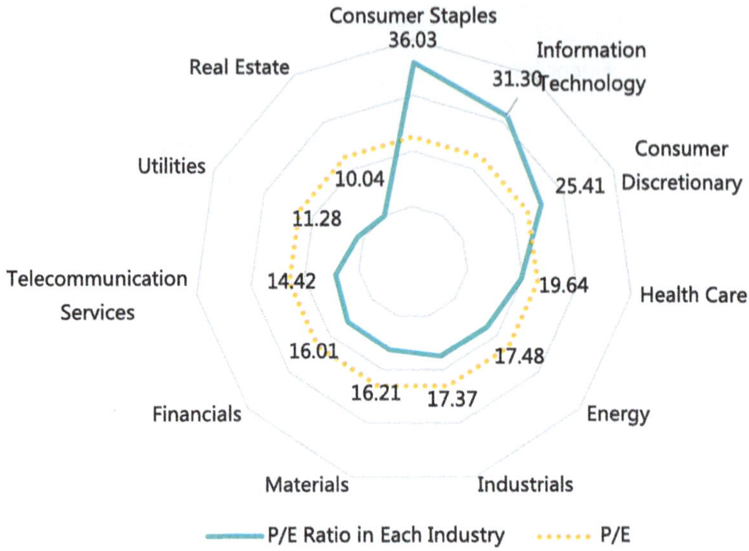


**Fig. 2.14** P/E of ZLCs in each industry (excluding loss-making companies) in 2017

**Table 2.2** Valuation of ZLCs in different industries[a]

| Industry | P/B ratio | P/S ratio | P/E ratio | P/E ratio (excluding loss-making companies) |
|---|---|---|---|---|
| Materials | 1.16 | 0.98 | 16.38 | 16.21 |
| Telecommunication services | 1.88 | 1.44 | 14.42 | 14.42 |
| Real estate | 1.17 | 0.56 | 10.04 | 10.04 |
| Industrials | 1.67 | 0.77 | 17.81 | 17.37 |
| Utilities | 0.86 | 1.84 | 11.28 | 11.28 |
| Financials | 0.97 | 0.24 | 16.69 | 16.01 |
| Consumer discretionary | 3.39 | 1.33 | 46.26 | 25.41 |
| Energy | 1.70 | 2.93 | 54.32 | 17.48 |
| Consumer staples | 1.81 | 1.54 | 38.71 | 36.03 |
| Information technology | 3.17 | 2.68 | 72.05 | 31.30 |
| Health care | 3.01 | 3.16 | 23.08 | 19.64 |
| Overall | 2.35 | 1.37 | 32.53 | 22.81 |

[a]Classified according to wind primary industry classification standard

The three valuation indicators of ZLCs in the Internet industry were significantly higher than those of non-Internet companies. This suggests that the capital market has much higher expectation on the Internet industry than the non-Internet industry (Tables 2.2 and 2.3).

**Table 2.3** Valuation of Internet and non-Internet ZLCs in 2017

| Industry | P/B ratio | P/S ratio | P/E ratio | P/E ratio (excluding loss-making companies) |
|---|---|---|---|---|
| Internet | 4.42 | 2.65 | 204.10 | 31.06 |
| Non-Internet | 1.96 | 1.14 | 24.08 | 21.12 |
| Entire level | 2.35 | 1.37 | 32.53 | 22.81 |

# Chapter 3
# Profitability of ZLCs in 2017

## 3.1 Revenue Quality Analysis

Revenue is the foundation and driving force for companies to survive and develop. With no revenue, a company will not be able to grow in a long run. Total revenue is the most direct indicator of revenue quality analysis, and changes in revenue can reflect the growth and volatility of a company's revenue.

### *3.1.1 Overall Status of Total Revenue*

In 2017, the total revenue of ZLCs reached 3988.6 billion yuan, representing an increase of 14% y-o-y. Due to the overall macroeconomic slowdown in China, the growth rate of the total revenue of ZLCs declined over the previous years, but still exceeded that of the total revenue of industrial enterprises above designated size (11.1%),[1] indicating that technological innovation-based companies of Zhongguancun enjoy a more sustainable growth (Fig. 3.1).

Domestic listed companies contributed a majority part of the total revenue of ZLCs, followed by HK listed companies and then U.S. listed companies. As for the growth rate, U.S. listed companies ranked first, followed by domestic companies and Hong Kong companies. To be specific, the revenue of domestic listed companies was 2191.4 billion yuan, accounting for 55% of the total and increasing by 14% y-o-y; the revenue of oversea listed companies was 1797.2 billion yuan, accounting for 45%. Among the oversea listed companies, the revenue of U.S. listed companies was 585.5 billion yuan, accounting for 15% of the total and rising 36% y-o-y; the revenue of HK listed companies was 1211.6 billion yuan, accounting for 30% of the total and increasing by 8% y-o-y (Fig. 3.2).

[1] Date source: China National Bureau of Statistics.



Zhongguancun Listed Companies Association, *The Competitiveness Report of Zhongguancun Listed Companies (2018)*,
https://doi.org/10.1007/978-981-13-7697-9_3

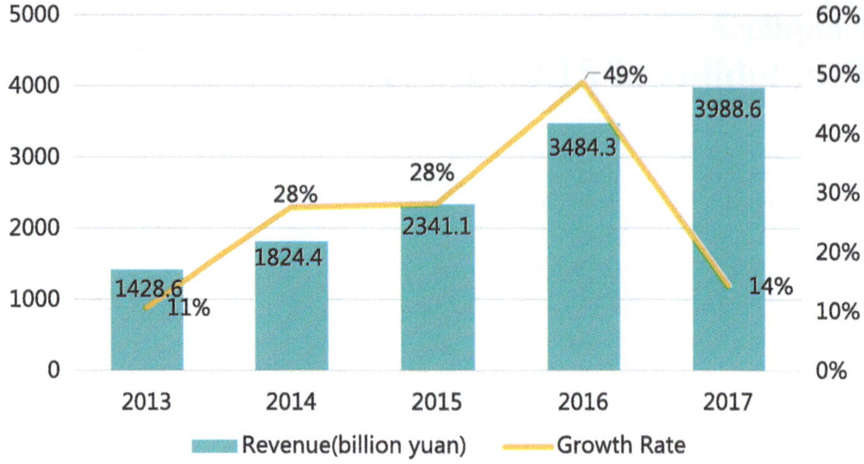


**Fig. 3.1** Revenue of ZLCs (2013–2017)

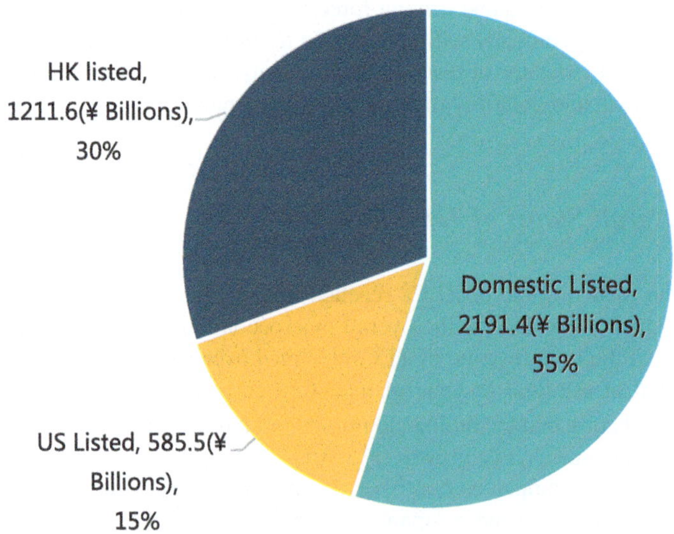


**Fig. 3.2** Composition of ZLCs' revenue in 2017

The total revenue of ZLCs reported a y-o-y growth of 504.3 billion yuan in 2017. The increase was mainly attributed to domestic listed companies. Out of the 504.3 billion yuan, 272 billion yuan (or 54% of the total) was from domestic listed companies, 232.3 billion yuan (46%) from overseas listed companies. Among overseas listed companies, U.S. listed companies enjoyed an increase of 153.5 billion yuan in revenue, accounting for 30% of the total and HK listed companies had an increment of 78.8 billion yuan in revenue, 16% of the total (Fig. 3.3).

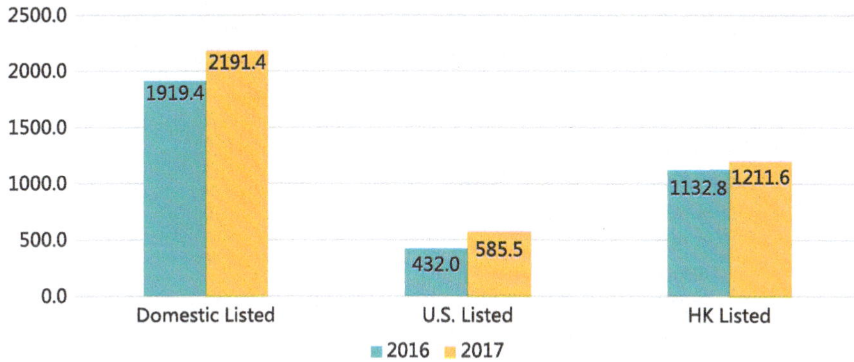


**Fig. 3.3** Revenue of ZLCs in each capital market (2016–2017) (¥ Billions)

### *3.1.2 Revenue Ranking*

In 2017, the total revenue of the top 30 ZLCs reached 3214.3 billion yuan, accounting for 81% of the total and increasing by 13% compared with 2016. Seven ZLCs reported a revenue of more than 100 billion yuan: China Railway, CCCC, Jingdong, Legend Holding, Lenovo Group, Baic Motor and CNBM. Only three of them—Jingdong, Baidu and Bluefocus—are Internet companies.

Compared with 2016, the ranking list of 30 ZLCs with highest revenue in 2017 did not change much except that LeTV and Guodian Technology & Environment were replaced by TDTEC and Bluefocus, respectively. The remaining 28 were on the list for two years, though in different orders. This indicates that the overall development of ZLCs, especially the leading ones, has been relatively stable (see Fig. 3.4).

The 30 ZLCs were mainly in three industries: Industrials (9), Information Technology (7) and Consumer Discretionary (6). The rest were in Materials (2), Telecommunication Services (1), Real Estate (1), Utilities (1), Financials (1), Consumer Staples (1), and Health Care (1).

Only three of the 30 ZLCs were Internet companies, namely Jingdong, Baidu and Bluefocus, and the remaining 27 were non-Internet companies.

### *3.1.3 Industry Distribution of Revenue*

In 2017, companies in Industrials, Information Technology and Consumer Discretionary[2] accounted for the majority of the total revenue of ZLCs. In fact, the revenue of the three sectors was 1534.5, 899.9, and 743.7 billion yuan, respectively. They contributed 80% of the total revenue. The average revenue of companies in

[2]Classified according to Wind Primary Industry Classification Standard.

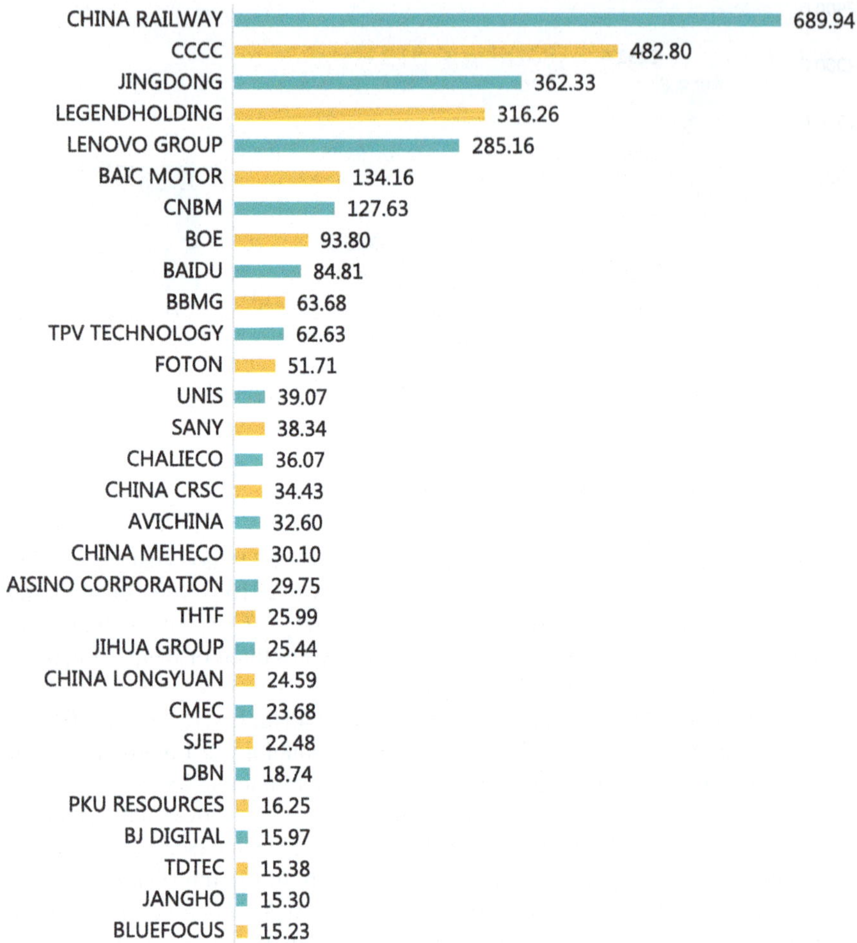


**Fig. 3.4** ZLCs with top 30 revenue in 2017 (¥ Billions)

Financials, Industrials, Consumer Discretionary, Telecommunication Services and Materials were higher than the total average (12.8 billion yuan) (Figs. 3.5 and 3.6).

The revenue of ZLCs in the non-Internet industry was as high as 3380.7 billion yuan, equalling 85% of the total, because they were a majority. In contrast, the revenue of Internet companies was only 607.9 billion yuan, accounting for 15.2%. However, the average revenue of non-Internet companies was 12.5 billion yuan, lower than the total average, while that of Internet companies was 14.8 billion yuan, beating the average (Table 3.1).

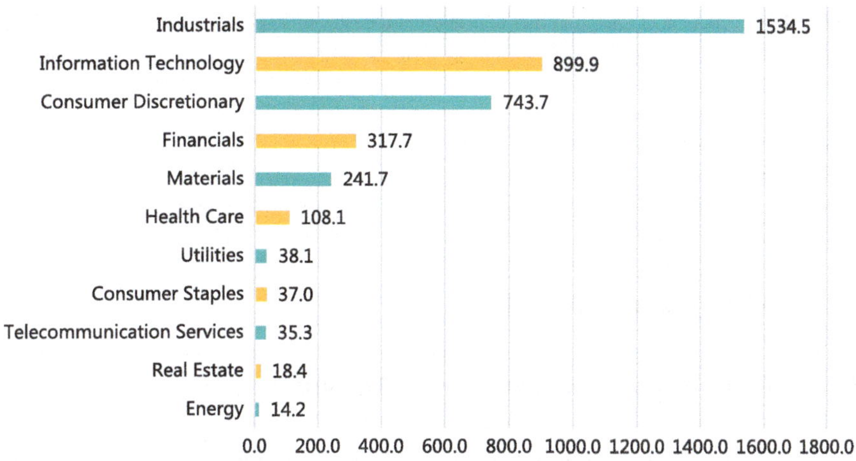


**Fig. 3.5** Revenue of ZLCs in each industry in 2017 (¥ Billions)

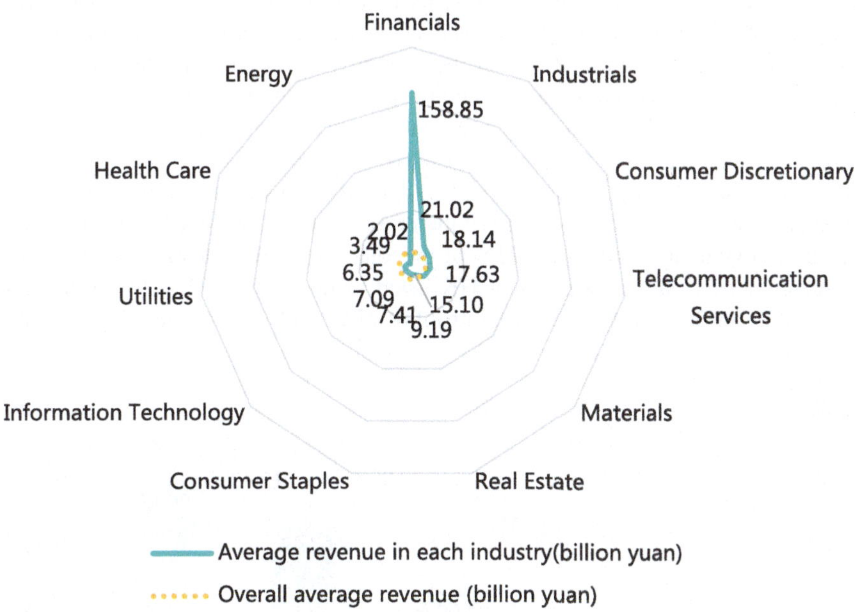


**Fig. 3.6** Average revenue of ZLCs in each industry in 2017

**Table 3.1** Revenue of ZLCs in internet/non-internet industry in 2017

| Industry | Revenue (billion yuan) | Proportion (%) | Number | Average revenue of each industry (billion yuan) |
|---|---|---|---|---|
| Non-internet | 3380.7 | 85 | 271 | 12.5 |
| Internet | 607.9 | 15 | 41 | 14.8 |

## 3.2 Profit Quality Analysis

### *3.2.1 Gross Profit and Gross Profit Margin*

The gross profit and gross profit margin of ZLCs continued to grow steadily. In 2017, the gross profit of ZLCs reached 803.5 billion yuan, rising by 126.4 billion yuan compared with 2016, which represents a y-o-y growth of 19%. The gross profit margin of ZLCs in 2017 was 20.14%. The increase in gross profit margin reveals that the operational efficiency of ZLCs has been improved to a certain extent (Fig. 3.7).

Domestic listed companies accounted for the largest proportion of gross profit of ZLCs, followed by HK listed companies and U.S. listed companies. The gross profit of U.S. listed companies saw the greatest y-o-y increase. Among them, the gross profit of domestic listed companies was 398.3 billion yuan, accounting for 50% of the total, with a y-o-y increase of 17%; the gross profit of U.S. listed companies was 173 billion yuan, accounting for 21% of the total gross profit of ZLC, with a y-o-y increase of 38%; the gross profit of HK listed companies was 232.2 billion yuan, accounting for 29% of the total gross profit of ZLC, with a y-o-y increase of 12%.

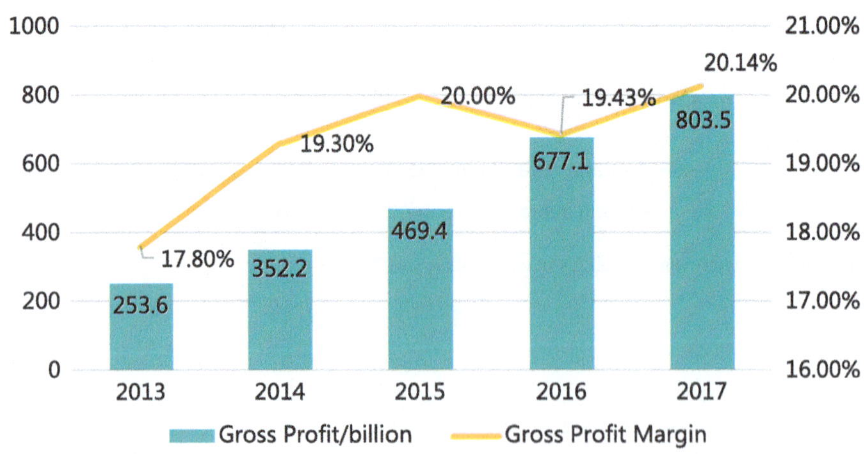


**Fig. 3.7** Gross profit and gross profit margin of ZLCs (2013–2017)

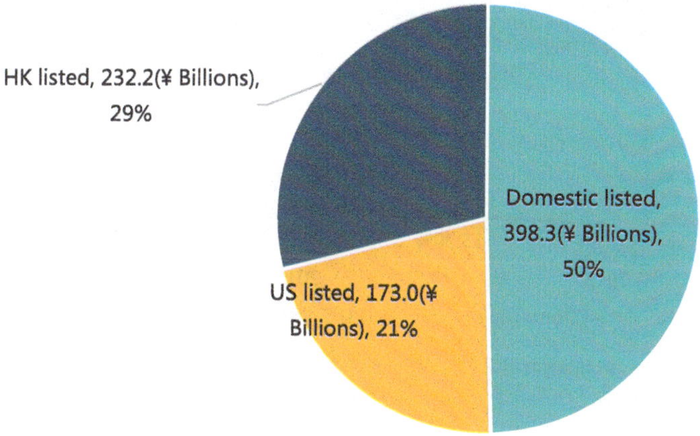


**Fig. 3.8** Composition of ZLCs' gross profit in 2017

**Fig. 3.9** Gross profit of ZLCs in each capital market (2016–2017) (¥ Billions)

The total gross profit of ZLCs increased by 126.4 billion yuan year on year in 2017. The growth is mainly attributed to domestic listed companies. The gross profit of domestic listed companies increased by 56.5 billion yuan, accounting for 44% of the total increment. Among overseas listed companies, U.S. listed companies saw an increment of 47.4 billion yuan in gross profit, equalling 37% of the total, while HK listed companies reported an increment of 24 billion yuan in gross profit, which was 19% of the total (Figs. 3.8 and 3.9).

The gross profit margin of U.S. listed companies was the highest in 2017 because many of them are highly profitable Internet companies. The profit margins of domestic and HK listed companies were very nearly the same. Besides, the profit margin of each capital market in 2017 slightly increased over 2016. The rather stable gross profit margin indicates that ZLCs grew quite steadily in 2017 (Fig. 3.10).

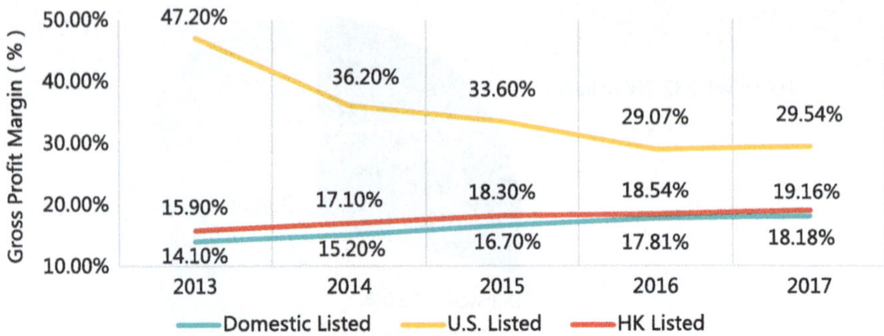


**Fig. 3.10** Gross profit margin of ZLCs in each capital market (2013–2017)

### *3.2.2 Rankings of Gross Profit and Gross Profit Margin*

The total gross profit of ZLCs on the top 30 ranking list of gross profit in 2017 reached 555.1 billion yuan, which accounted for 69% of the total gross profit of ZLCs. Compared with 2016, the top 30 companies' gross profit increased by 18%. Among them, there were 11 ZLCs with a gross profit of more than 10 billion yuan. They were CCCC, China Railway, Jingdong, Legend Holdings, Baidu, Lenovo Group, Baic Motor, CNBM, BOE, BBMG and SANY (in a descending order in terms of gross profit). Among them, the top three companies were CCCC, China Railway and Jingdong, and eight were Internet companies. New Oriental Education & Technology, Weibo, Bitauto, Tal Education, Autohome and DFYL were newly included on the list. The ranking of New Oriental Education & Technology rose significantly, jumping from 82nd in 2016 to 18th in 2017 (see Fig. 3.11).

The top 30 ZLCs were mainly in three industries: Information Technology (13), Industrials (6), Consumer Discretionary (5). The rest were in Materials (2), Utilities (1), Financials (1), Telecommunication Services (1) and Health Care (1). Eight Internet companies were on the list in 2017, namely Baidu, 58.com, SINA, Weibo, Bitauto, SOHU.Com, Autohome and Jingdong, and the remaining 22 were non-Internet companies.

In 2017, on the ranking list of gross profit margin, the top 30 ZLCs had gross margins of over 65%. Six companies reported gross margins of more than 90%. They were Beigene (97.91%), C Health GP (96.45%), Staidson Bio (94.45%) from the Health Care industry, Glodon (93.07%), 58.com (90.81%) and Jianpu Technology (90.05%) from the Information Technology industry (in brackets are the company's gross profit margin). The 30 companies were mainly in two industries—eleven were in Health Care and sixteen were in Information Technology. And the rest three were in Consumer Discretionary, Financials, and Industrials. The distribution results from the attributes of different industries. The technical threshold of Health Care and Information Technology is relatively high because of patent regulations, and thus companies in the two industries have greater core competitiveness. That's why those companies often have high gross profit margin (Fig. 3.12).

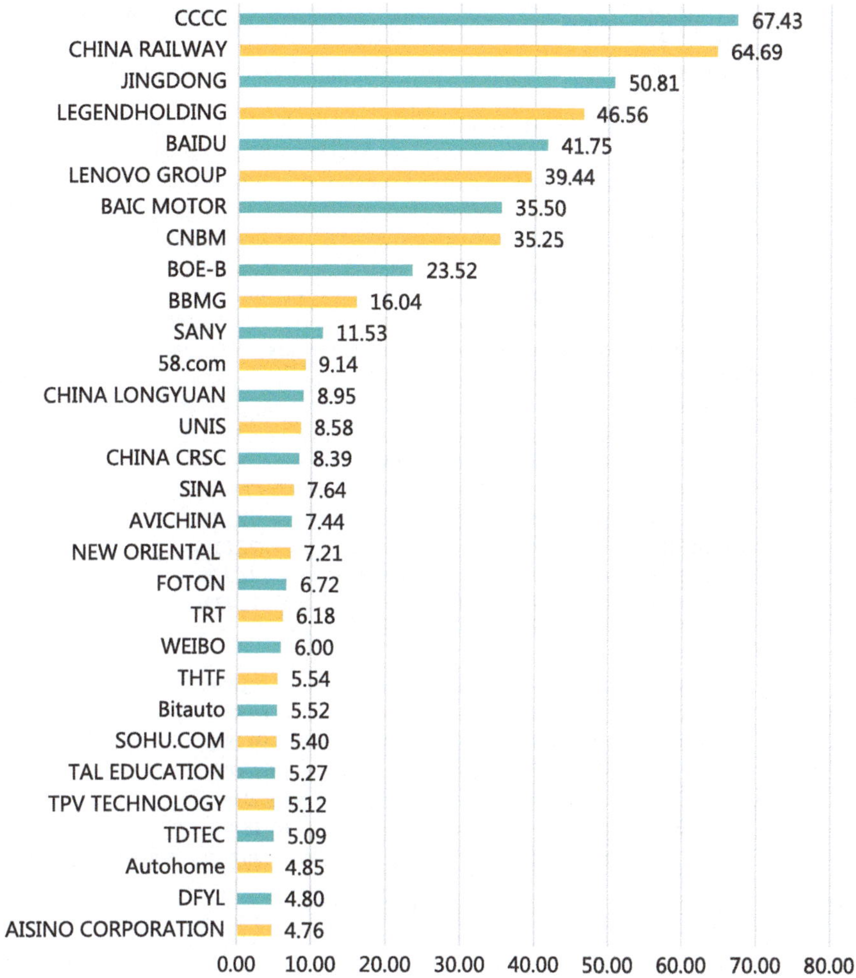


**Fig. 3.11** 30 ZLCs with greatest gross profit in 2017 (¥ Billions)

### 3.2.3 *Gross Profit and Gross Profit Margin of Companies in Different Industries*

The gross profits of companies from IT, Industrials and Consumer Discretionary were 254.1, 216.6, and 139.6 billion yuan, respectively. Altogether, they accounted for a majority of the total gross profit of ZLCs (Fig. 3.13).

The average gross profits of companies in five industries—Financials, Telecommunications Services, Materials, Consumer Discretionary and Industrials—were higher than the total average (2.5 billion yuan). The average gross profit margins of seven industries—Utilities, Health Care, Energy, Consumer Staples, Informa-

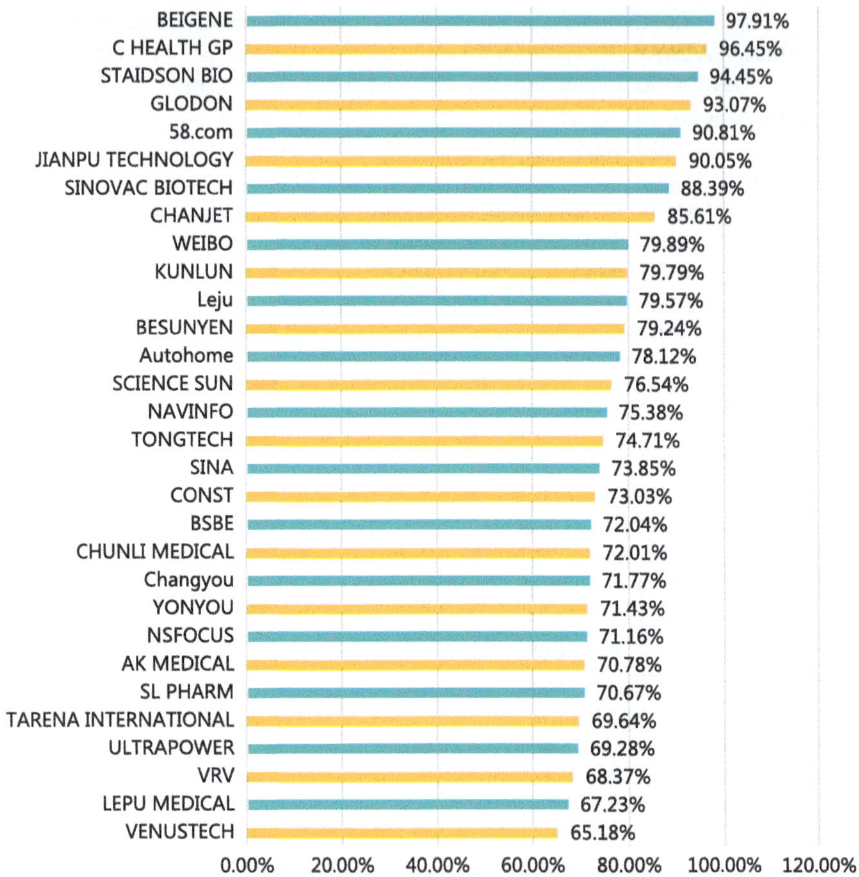


**Fig. 3.12** ZLCs with top 30 gross profit margins in 2017

tion Technology, Materials and Telecommunications Services—were higher than the overall average (20.14%) (Figs. 3.14 and 3.15).

The total gross profit of ZLCs in the non-Internet industry was as high as 637.9 billion yuan, equalling 79% of the total, because they were a majority. In contrast, the total gross profit of Internet companies was only 165.6 billion yuan, accounting for 21%. However, the average gross profit of Internet companies was 4.04 billion yuan, beating than the total average, while that of non-Internet companies was 2.35 billion yuan, lower than the average. The average gross profit margin of Internet companies (27.2%) was much higher than that of non-Internet companies (18.9%) (Table 3.2).

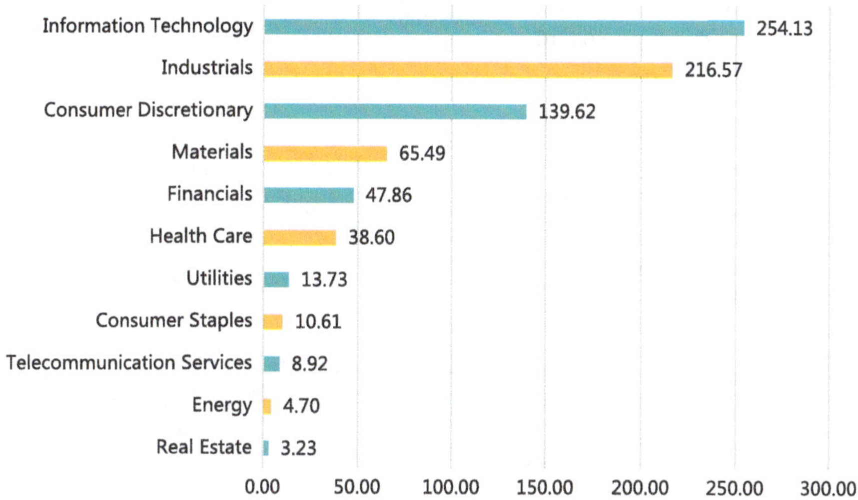


**Fig. 3.13** Gross profit of ZLCs in each industry in 2017 (¥ Billions)

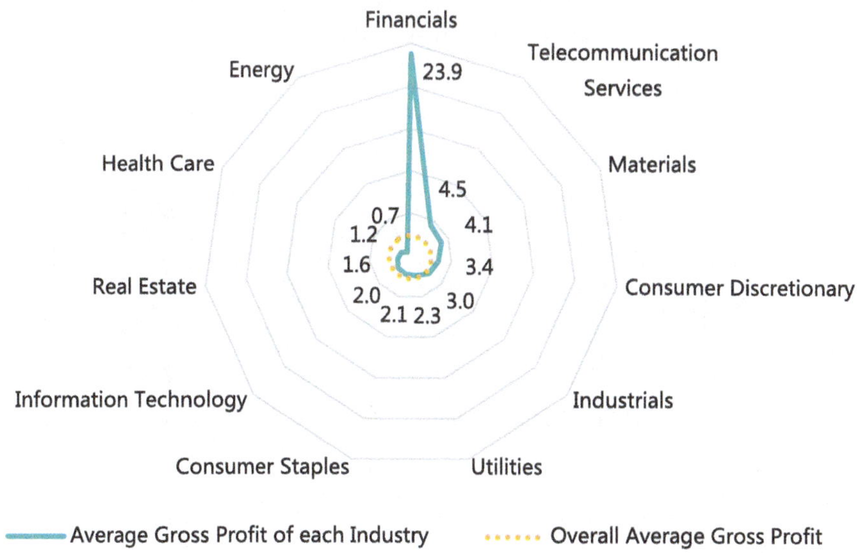


**Fig. 3.14** Average gross profit of ZLCs in each industry in 2017 (¥ Billions)

**Table 3.2** Gross profit and gross profit margin of ZLCs in internet/non-internet industry in 2017

| Industry | Gross profit (billion yuan) | Average gross profit (billion yuan) | Average gross profit margin (%) |
|---|---|---|---|
| Non-internet | 165.6 | 4.04 | 27.2 |
| Internet | 637.9 | 2.35 | 18.9 |
| Overall | 803.5 | 2.58 | 20.1 |

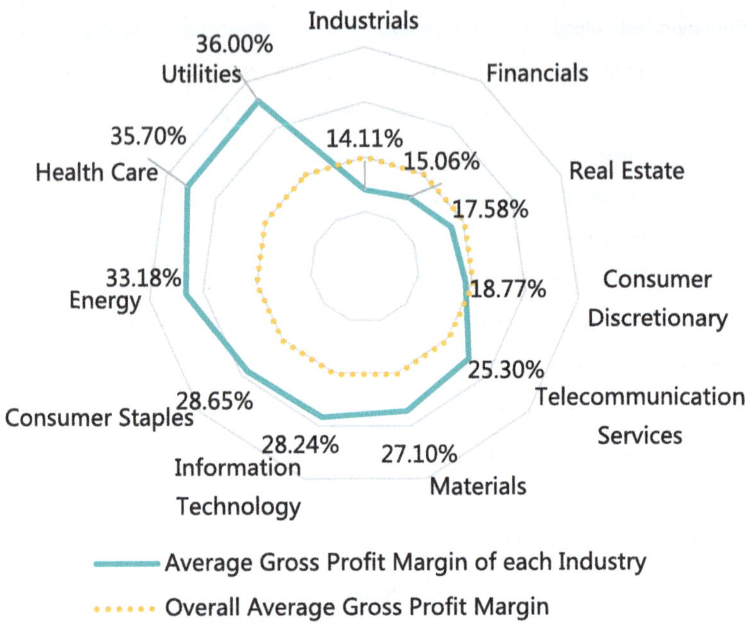


**Fig. 3.15** Average gross profit margin of ZLCs in each industry in 2017

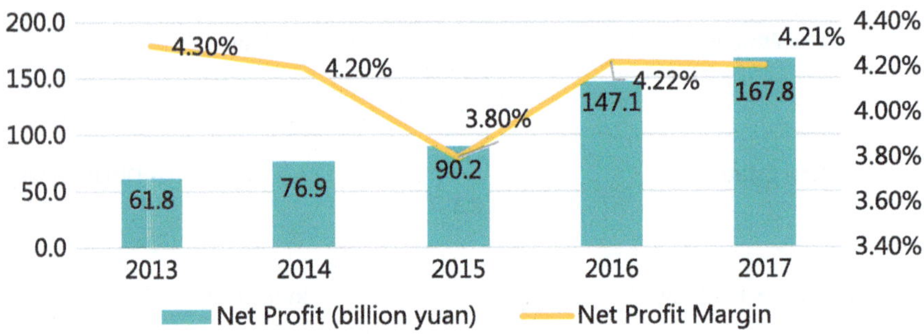


**Fig. 3.16** Net profit and net profit margin of ZLCs (2013–2017)

### *3.2.4 Net Profit and Net Profit Margin*

In 2017, the total net profit of ZLCs increased by 20.7 billion yuan compared with 2016, reaching 167.8 billion yuan, which represents a y-o-y increase of 14%, and the total net profit attributable to the parent company was 147 billion yuan. The number of profitable companies was 263, accounting for 84% of the total, and the net profit of those companies was 206.6 billion yuan; the remaining 49 companies, which was 16% of the total, suffered losses of 38.9 billion yuan. Compared with 2016, the net profit margin of ZLCs in 2017 barely changed (Fig. 3.16).

Among the 263 profitable ZLCs, there were 201 domestic listed companies, 41 HK listed companies, and 21 U.S. listed companies. In other words, 91% of domestic listed companies, 79% of HK listed companies and 53% of US listed companies achieved profitability. Due to different regulations in different capital markets, the proportion of profitable companies in domestic listed companies was greater than those in HK listed companies and U.S. listed companies.

Domestic listed companies accounted most (more than 50%) for the total net profit of ZLCs, and HK listed companies, US listed companies followed. The net profit of US listed companies increased the most. The net profit of domestic listed companies was 94.1 billion yuan, taking up 56% of the total and representing a y-o-y increase of 1%; the net profit of US listed companies was 24.7 billion yuan, 15% of the total, a y-o-y increase of 157%; the net profit of HK listed companies was 49 billion yuan, 29% of the total, a y-o-y increase of 11%. Although the proportion of profitable companies in US listed companies was relatively low, the net profit of leading Internet companies increased significantly. In 2017, there were seven U.S. listed companies whose net profit rose by more than 1 billion yuan. All of them are Internet companies. They are Baidu (net profit growth: 6.7 billion yuan, a y-o-y increase of 57%), Jingdong (net profit growth: 3.8 billion yuan, a y-o-y increase of 100%), 58.com (net profit growth: 2.2 billion yuan, a y-o-y increase of 277%), Weibo (net profit growth: 1.5 billion yuan, a y-o-y increase of 205%),Cheetah Mobile (net profit growth: 1.5 billion yuan, a y-o-y increase of 1808%), FANG (net profit growth: 1.3 billion Yuan, a y-o-y increase of 112%), Momo (net profit growth: 1.1 billion yuan, a y-o-y increase of 106%) (Fig. 3.17 and 3.18).

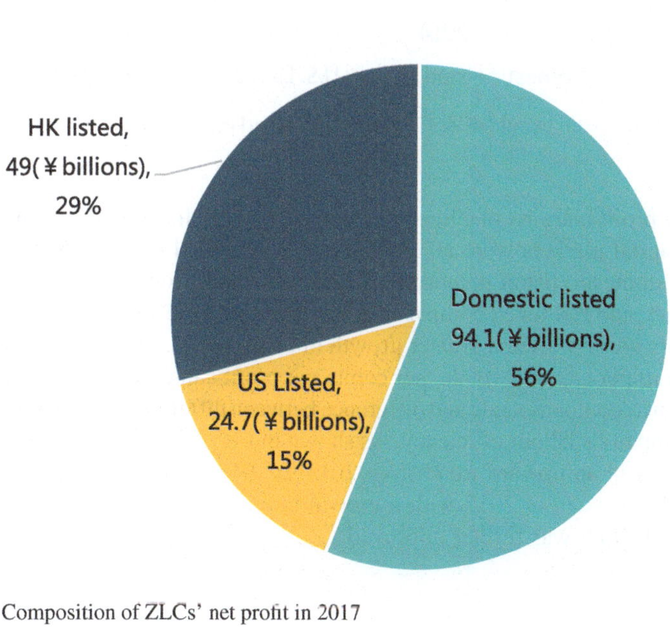


**Fig. 3.17** Composition of ZLCs' net profit in 2017

**Fig. 3.18** Net profit of ZLC in each capital market (2016–2017) (Unit: billion)

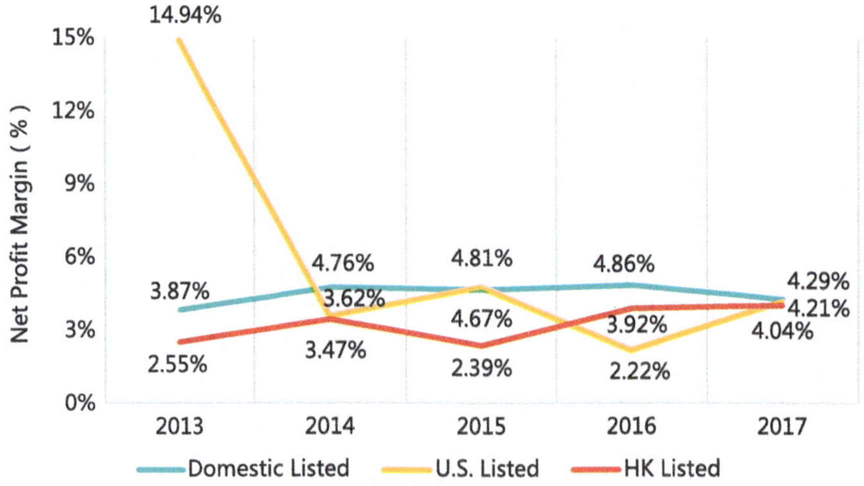


**Fig. 3.19** The net profit margin of ZLC in each capital market (2013–2017)

The net profit margins of Zhongguancun companies listed in the domestic, U.S. and HK capital markets were all close to 4%. Compared with 2016, the net profit margin of domestic listed companies slightly dropped from 4.86 to 4.29%, while those of U.S. and HK listed companies both increased. The net profit margin of U.S. listed companies reported a greater growth of 90% (Fig. 3.19).

Similar to per capita revenue, per capita net profit can eliminate the influence of factors such as company scale and difference between different industries and directly show a company's labour efficiency. As shown in Fig. 3.20, the per capita net profit of ZLCs was in an upward trend from 2013 to 2017. It rose from 75,700 yuan in 2016 to 81,800 yuan in 2017 with a growth rate of 8%, indicating that the labour efficiency of ZLCs was further improved.

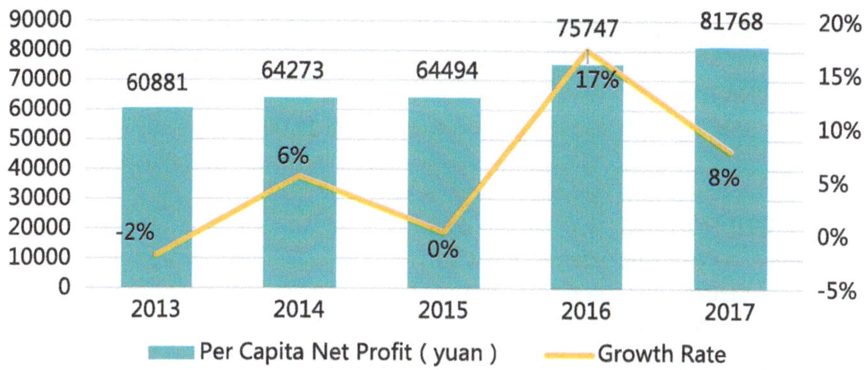


**Fig. 3.20** Per captia net profit of ZLCs (2013–2017)

### *3.2.5 Rankings of Net Profit and Net Profit Margin*

The total net profit of ZLCs on the top 30 ranking list of net profit in 2017 reached 141.3 billion yuan, making up 84.2% of the total net profit of ZLCs. Compared with 2016, the top 30 companies' net profit increased by 21.8%. Among them, there were four ZLCs with a net profit of more than 10 billion yuan. They were CCCC, Baidu, China Railway and Baic Motor. CCCC and China Railway ranked top three on the three list of revenue, gross profit and net profit. Seven companies, Kingsoft, Golden Meditech, UNIS, Weibo, Sina, Sany and Momo were newly included on the list of net profit in 2017 (Fig. 3.21).

The top 30 ZLCs were mainly in two industries: Information Technology (12) and Industrials (9). The rest were in Healthcare (3), Materials (3), Consumer Discretionary (2), Financials (1), Utilities (1), and Telecommunications Services (1). Five Internet companies were on the list in 2017, namely Baidu, Weibo, Sina, Momo and Autohome, and the remaining 25 were non-Internet companies.

On the net profit margin ranking[3] of 2017, the top 30 ZLCs had a net profit margin of more than 20%. There were six companies with a net profit margin of over 50%. They were Sinovels (net profit margin: 81.59%) from Industrials, BTBP (net profit margin: 70.59%), PW Medtech (net profit margin: 52.75%), C Health GP (net profit margin: 52.07%) from Health Care, and Kingsoft (net profit margin: 63.63%), New Sports (net profit margin: 53.18%) from Information Technology (Fig. 3.22).

[3]In 2017, the net profit margin of Golden Meditech was as high as 1341.38%, which was regarded as an abnormal value. Therefore, the company was excluded from the ranking. In 2017, the company's continuing businesses lost 600 million yuan, and the annual profit from its discontinued business was 3.4 billion yuan, which was mainly attributed to the sale of International Cord Blood Bank Enterprise Group (GCBC).

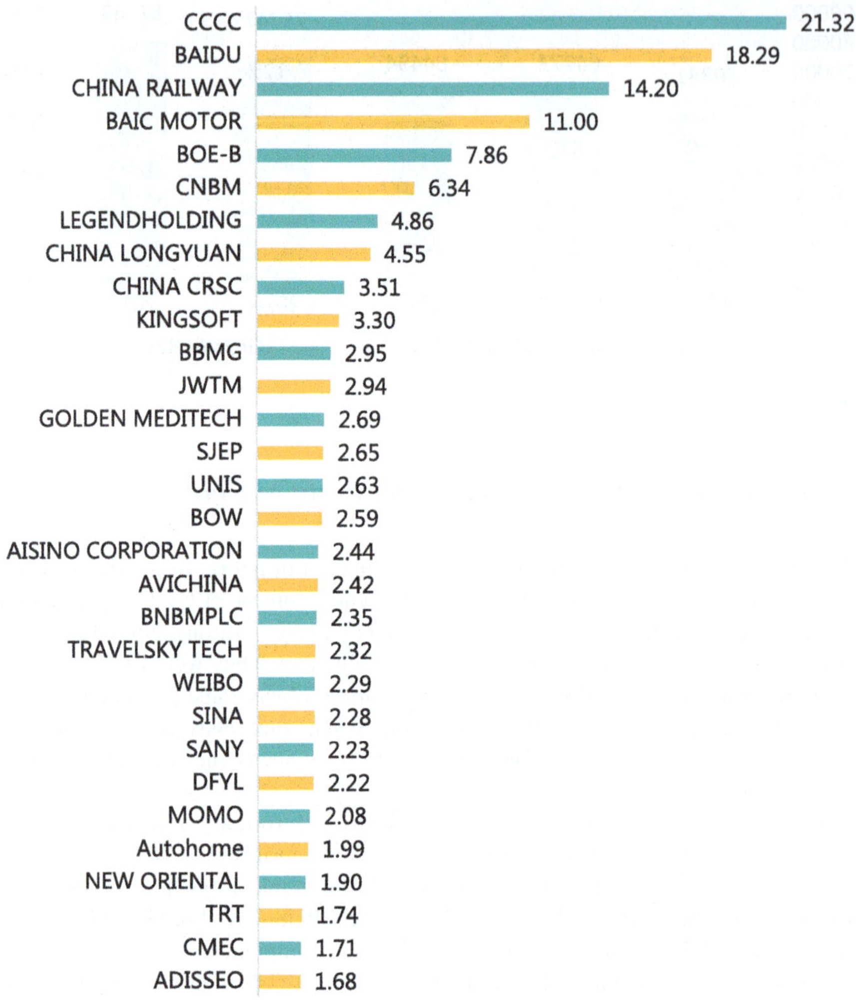


**Fig. 3.21** ZLCs with top 30 net profit in 2017 (¥ Billions)

### *3.2.6 Industry Distribution of Net Profit and Net Profit Margin*

In 2017, ZLCs in Industrials reported the highest total net profit of 66.1 billion yuan, followed by those in Information Technology (total net profit: 33.4 billion yuan) and Consumer Discretionary (total net profit: 21.3 billion yuan). The net profits of companies in these three industries accounted for 72% of the total. In terms of average net profit, five industries—Financials, Telecommunications Services, Utilities, Industrials and Materials—were higher than the overall average (500 million yuan).

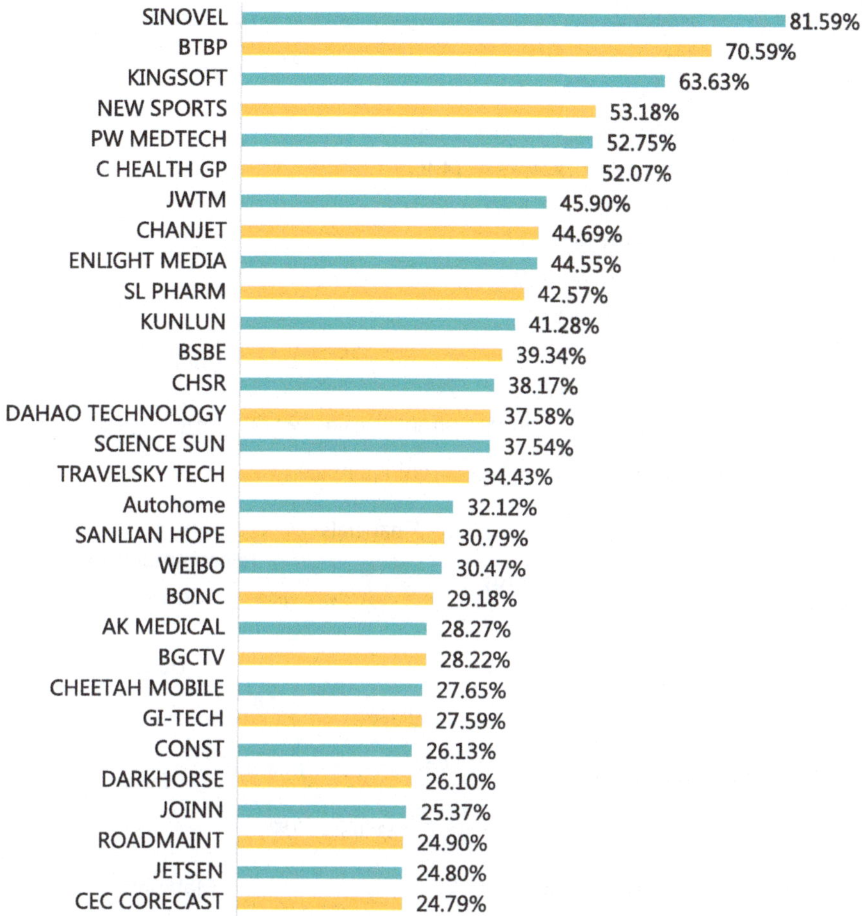


**Fig. 3.22** ZLCs with top 30 net profit margin in 2017

The average net profit of ZLCs in the Information Technology industry was lower than the overall average due to the huge loss worth 18.2 billion yuan of LeTV and high R&D spending. The average net profit margins of companies in seven industries, namely Utilities, Health Care, Telecommunications Services, Materials, Real estate, Energy and Industrials, were higher than the overall average (4.21%) (Figs. 3.23, 3.24 and 3.25).

The net profit of ZLCs in non-Internet industry in 2017 was as high as 159.9 billion yuan, accounting for 95% of the total, because they were a majority. In contrast, the revenue of Internet companies was only 7.9 billion yuan, accounting for 5%. The average net profit and net profit margin of Internet companies were 192 million yuan and 1.30%, which were much lower than the 590 million yuan and 4.73% of non-Internet companies. Besides the huge loss of LeTV in 2017, another more prevailing

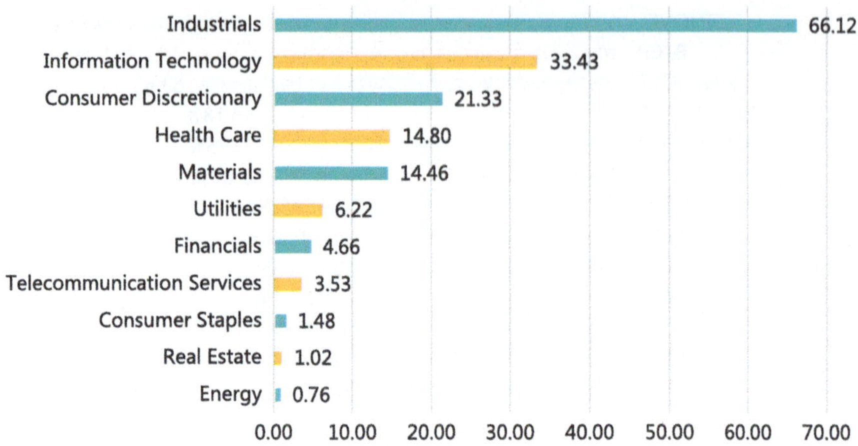


**Fig. 3.23** Net profit of ZLCs in each industry in 2017 (¥ Billions)

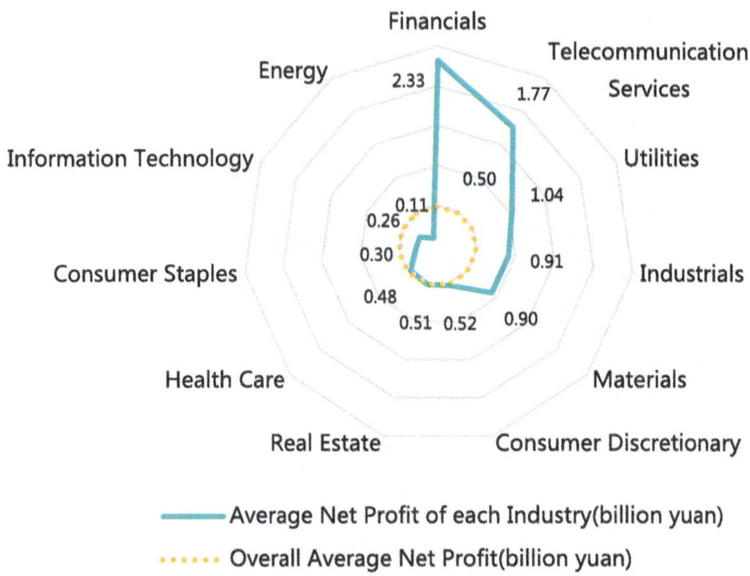


**Fig. 3.24** Average net profit of ZLCs in each industry in 2017

reason would be that it often takes a long time for an Internet company to reach profitability. In 2017, 38% of ZLCs in the Internet industry (16 companies) were unprofitable, while only 12% of non-Internet ZLCs (33 companies) hadn't achieved profitability (Table 3.3).

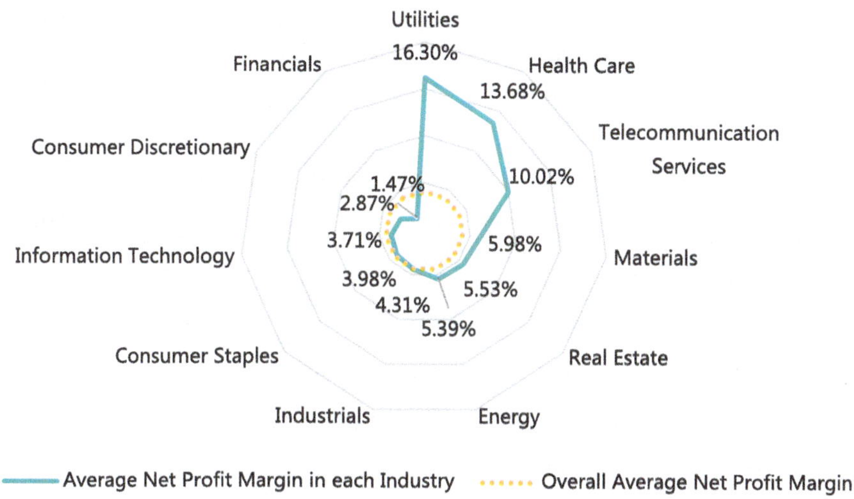


**Fig. 3.25** Average net profit margin of ZLCs in each industry in 2017

**Table 3.3** Net profit and net profit margin of ZLCs in internet/non-internet industry in 2017

| Industry | Net profit (billion yuan) | Average net profit (billion yuan) | Average net profit margin (%) |
|---|---|---|---|
| Non-internet | 7.9 | 0.192 | 1.30 |
| Internet | 159.9 | 0.590 | 4.73 |
| Overall | 167.8 | 0.538 | 4.21 |

*Remarks* With LeTV excluded, the total net profit of ZLCs in the Internet industry would be 26.1 billion yuan. The average net profit and profit margin of those companies would be 652 million yuan and 4.34%

## 3.3 Analysis on Profitability Ratios

### *3.3.1 Return on Assets*

Return on assets (ROA)[4]is an indicator that measures how much net profit each unit asset creates, namely the input-output ratio of financial resources. The higher the indicator, the more efficient the utilization of the enterprise assets, which indicates that the enterprise performs well in increasing income and/or saving capital.

In 2017, the return on assets of ZLCs was 2.77%, representing a y-o-y decrease of 16.27%. The main reason for the decline is that compared with 2016, the y-o-y growth rate of net profit of ZLCs in 2017 (14%) was lower than the y-o-y growth

[4]Return on Assets (ROA) = Net Profit/Average Total Assets.

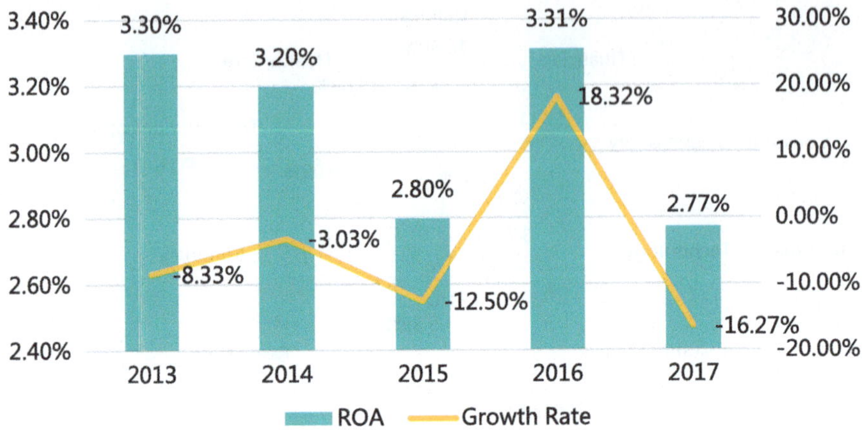


**Fig. 3.26** ROA of ZLCs (2013–2017)

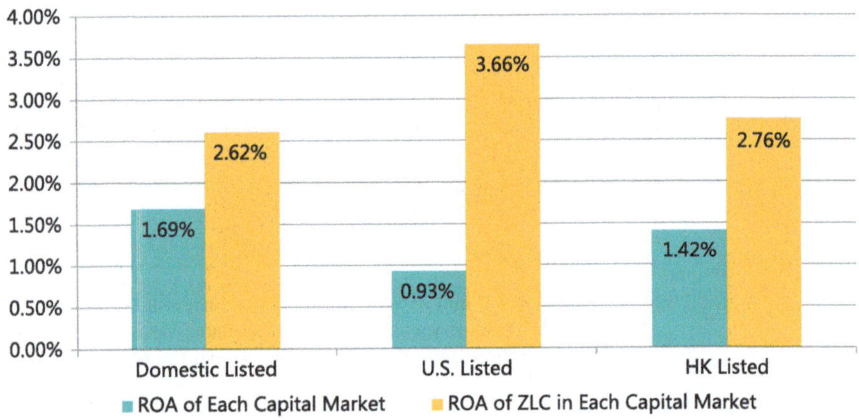


**Fig. 3.27** ROA between ZLCs and all companies in each capital market in 2017

rate of their average total assets (36%). Even so, the ROA of ZLCs in 2017 was still higher than that of all companies listed on the A-shares market (1.69%) (Fig. 3.26).

In 2017, the ROA of Zhongguancun companies listed in the Chinese mainland, Hong Kong and the U.S. were 2.62, 2.76 and 3.66%, respectively. Overall, the ROA of U.S. listed ZLCs was higher than those of HK listed companies and domestic listed companies (Fig. 3.27).

In each capital market, the ROA of Zhongguancun companies beat that of that of the overall market.

In 2017, the ROA of ZLCs in the Health Care industry was the highest, reaching 9.17%; the ROA of ZLCs in the Telecommunications Service industry was 6.06%, ranking the second. The indicators of ZLCs in Consumer Discretionary, Consumer Staples, and Industrials were higher than the overall average, while those of ZLCs

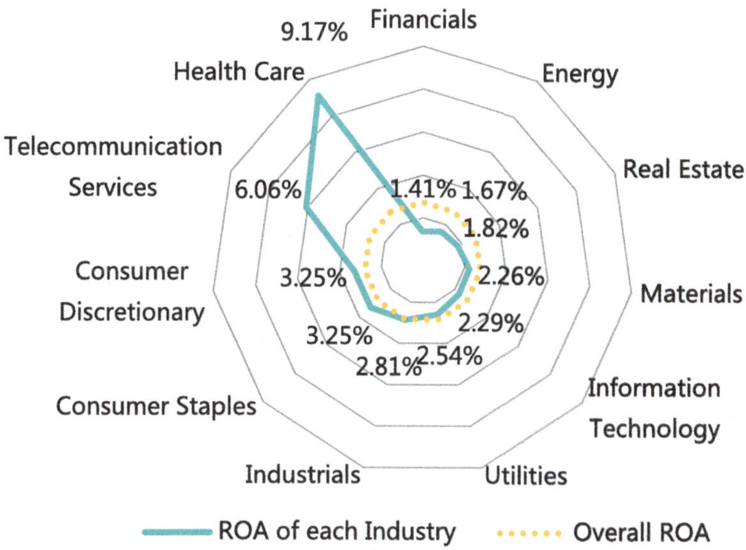


**Fig. 3.28** ROA of ZLCs in each industry in 2017

in Financials, Energy, Real Estate, Materials, Information Technology, and Utilities industries were slightly lower than the overall average (Fig. 3.28).

The ROA of ZLCs in the Internet industry was 1.10%, lower than that of ZLCs in the non-Internet industry (3.00%).

### *3.3.2 Return on Equity*

Return on equity (ROE)[5] measures the return on shareholders' equity and evaluates the efficiency of a company in using its net assets. The higher the ROE number, the higher the return of investment. In 2017, the ROE of ZLCs was 7.77%, decreasing by 22.22% y-o-y (Fig. 3.29).

In 2017, the ROE of Zhongguancun companies listed in the Chinese mainland, Hong Kong and the U.S. were 7.51, 8.57 and 7.81%, respectively. Overall, the ROE of HK listed ZLCs was higher than those of U.S. listed companies and domestic listed companies (Fig. 3.30).

In each capital market, the ROE of Zhongguancun companies was slightly lower than that of the overall market.

In 2017, the ZLCs in the Health Care industry reported the highest ROE of 13.84%, followed by companies in Telecommunications Service (13.56%), Indus-

[5]ROE = Net Profit Attributable to the Parent Company/Average Shareholder's Equity Attributable to the Parent Company.

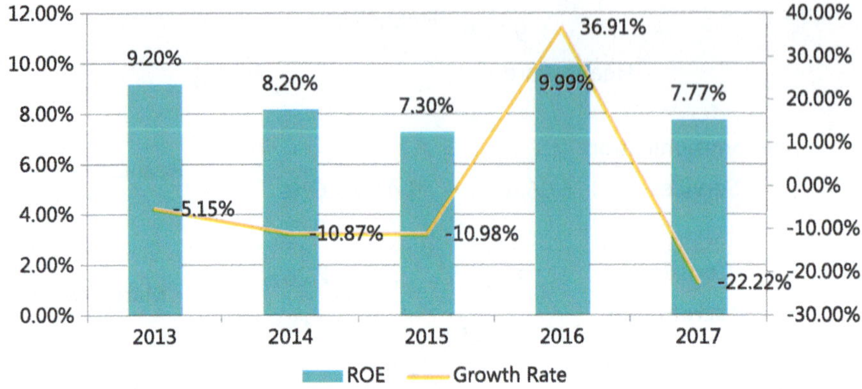


**Fig. 3.29** ROE of ZLCs (2013–2017)

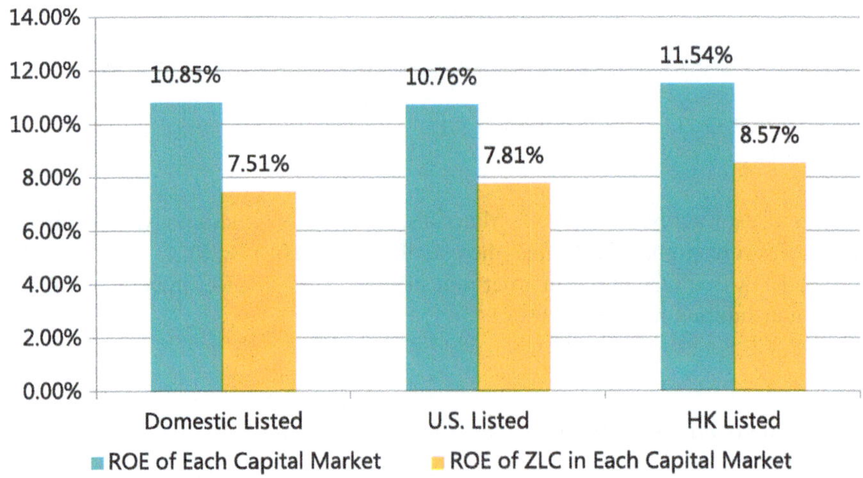


**Fig. 3.30** ROE of ZLCs and each capital market in 2017

trials (10.92%) and Real Estate (10.57%). The ROE of ZLCs in Health Care and Telecommunications Service were much higher than that of all ZLCs, while the indicators of ZLCs in Energy, Consumer Discretionary and Information Technology were slightly lower (Fig. 3.31).

The ROE of ZLCs in the non-Internet industry was 8.67%, and that of ZLCs in the Internet industry was 3.19%.

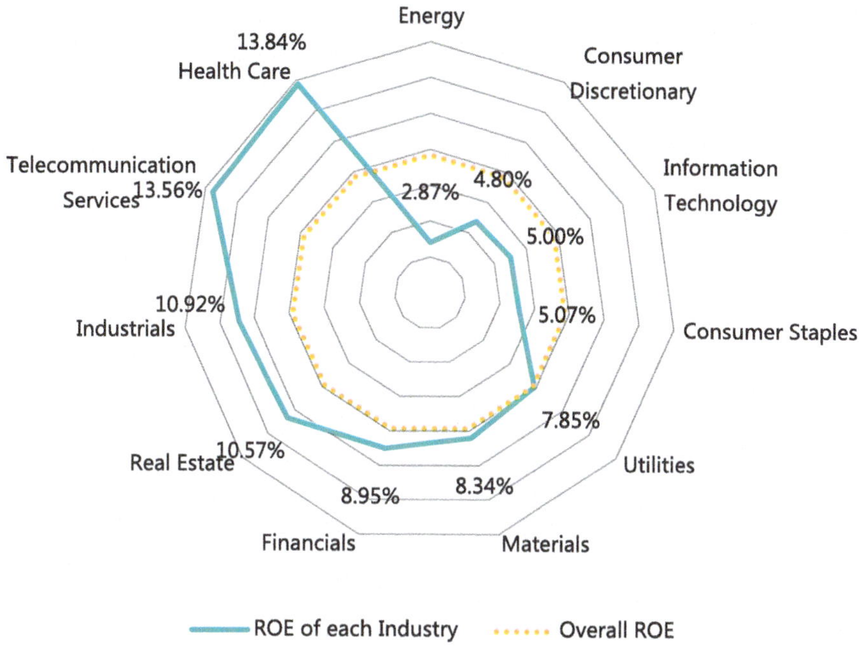


**Fig. 3.31** ROE of ZLCs in each industry in 2017

# Chapter 4
# Debt Paying Abilities of ZLCs in 2017

## 4.1 Assets Analysis

### *4.1.1 Overall Assets*

In 2017, the total assets of ZLCs reached 6379 billion yuan, representing a y-o-y increase of 12%. Compared with the previous four years, the growth rate of total assets has slowed down. The main reason was that the growth rate of newly listed companies in Zhongguancun has slowed down. In 2017, the number of newly listed companies increased by 9% y-o-y, while in 2016 this figure was 21% (Fig. 4.1).

Compared with 2016, the proportions of the total assets of ZLCs in different capital markets did not change significantly. Domestic listed companies still accounted for more than half of the total, followed by HK listed companies and US listed companies. In 2017, the assets of domestic listed companies were worth 3805.5 billion yuan, accounting for 60% of the total assets of ZLCs; the assets of HK listed companies were worth 1811.8 billion yuan, accounting for 28%; the assets of US listed companies were worth 761.7 billion yuan, accounting for 12% (Fig. 4.2).

From 2013 to 2017, the assets of ZLCs in all capital markets were increasing, but the growth rates were slowing down, which was consistent with the trend of ZLCs'

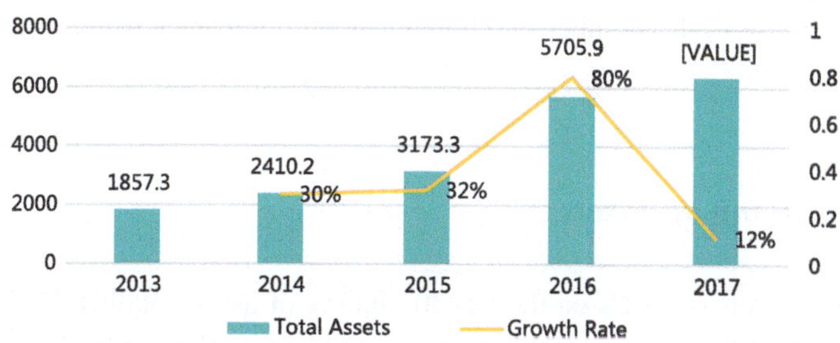


**Fig. 4.1** Total assets of ZLCs in 2013–2017 (Unit: ¥ billions)



Zhongguancun Listed Companies Association, *The Competitiveness Report of Zhongguancun Listed Companies (2018)*,
https://doi.org/10.1007/978-981-13-7697-9_4

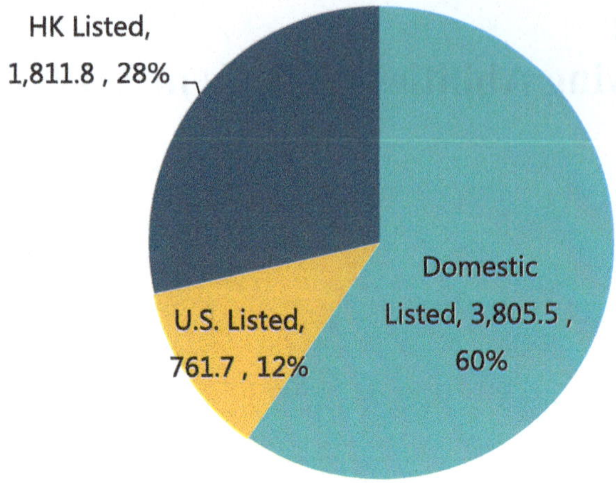


**Fig. 4.2** Assets of ZLC in different capital markets in 2017 (¥ billions)

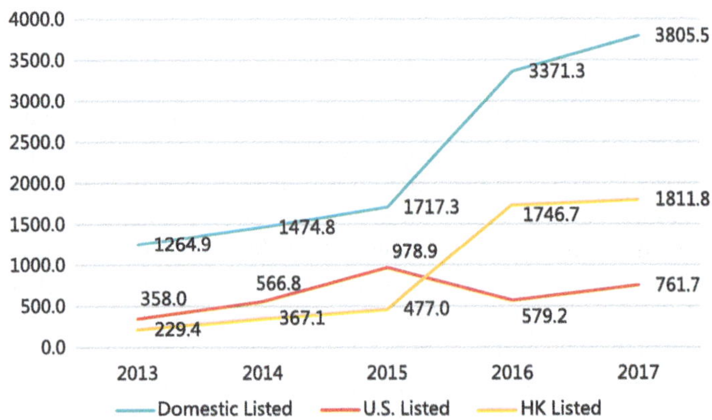


**Fig. 4.3** Assets of ZLCs in different capital markets (2013–2017) (¥ billions)

total assets. It was worth noting that in 2016, the assets of Zhongguancun companies listed in HK started to exceed those of US listed companies, mainly because of the gradual decrease in the number of Zhongguancun companies listed in the United States (Fig. 4.3).

### *4.1.2 Ranking of Assets*

In 2017, the assets of ZLCs on the top 30 ranking of assets totalled 4717.3 billion yuan, accounting for 73.95% of the total assets of ZLCs. The assets of the company that ranked 30th was 31.4 billion yuan. There were 11 companies whose assets exceeded 100 billion yuan. Different from the top 30 ranking in 2016, DFYL was included but LeTV was not in 2017. LeTV's total assets were worth 17.9 billion yuan in 2017, decreasing by 14.3 billion yuan compared with the previous year, which represents a y-o-y decline of 80%. The decline is largely resulted from to the company's significant provision for the impairment of inventories, trade receivables, intangible assets, etc., and its disposal of some fixed assets. In 2017, the total assets of DFYL reached 35.1 billion yuan, rising by 46% y-o-y. The growth mainly came from Construction Work-in-Progress, which was generated by the company's PPP projects. The asset account increased by 310% over the previous year (Fig. 4.4).

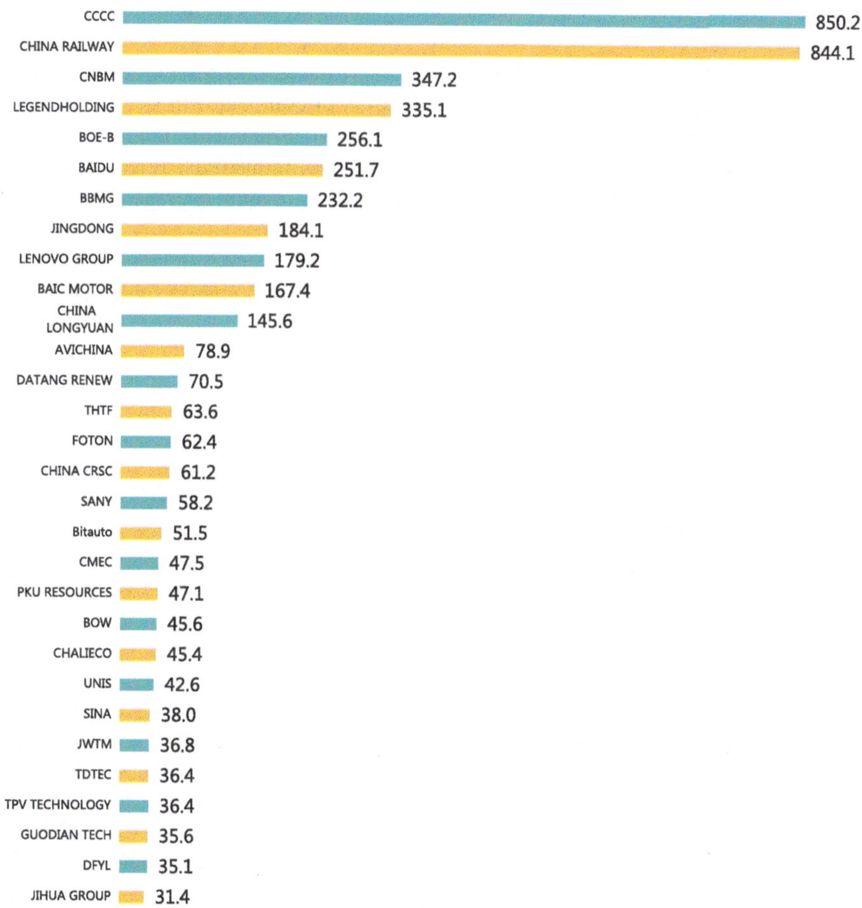


**Fig. 4.4** Top 30 ZLCs by assets in 2017 (¥ billions)

### *4.1.3 Industry Distribution of Assets*

The assets of ZLCs in Industrials accounted for the largest proportion (38%) of total 2017, reaching 2458.4 billion yuan. The second largest part was the assets of companies in Information Technology. Their assets were worth 1589.6 billion yuan, accounting for 25%. The third was companies in the Consumer Discretionary industry. Their assets totalled 695.5 billion yuan, accounting for 11%. The distribution of the total assets reflects that most ZLCs are concentrated in three key industries: Industrials and Information Technology industry, which are two industries bolstered by modern science and technology, and Consumer Discretionary, the core of the tertiary industry. It can be thus concluded that ZLCs have relatively advanced productivity at the industrial level.

However, ZLCs in Financials have the greatest total assets on average, which was worth 168.5 billion yuan. The average total assets of companies in Utilities was 42 billion yuan, ranking the second. The third was in Materials, with the average total assets reaching 41.2 billion yuan. The average assets of Industrials, Telecommunications Services and Real Estate were also higher than the overall average (20.4 billion yuan) (Figs. 4.5 and 4.6).

The average assets of non-Internet ZLCs was worth 20.6 billion yuan, which was slightly higher than that of Internet companies (19.5 billion yuan) (Table 4.1).

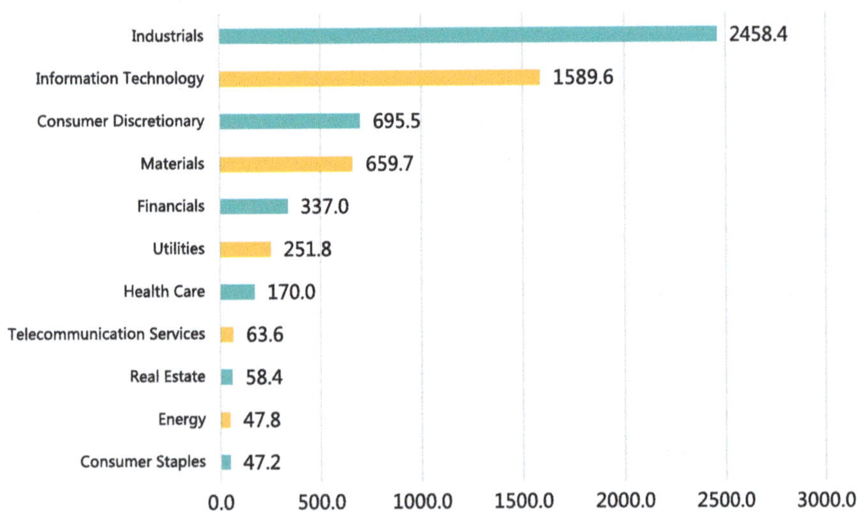


**Fig. 4.5** Assets of ZLCs in each industry in 2017 (¥ billions)

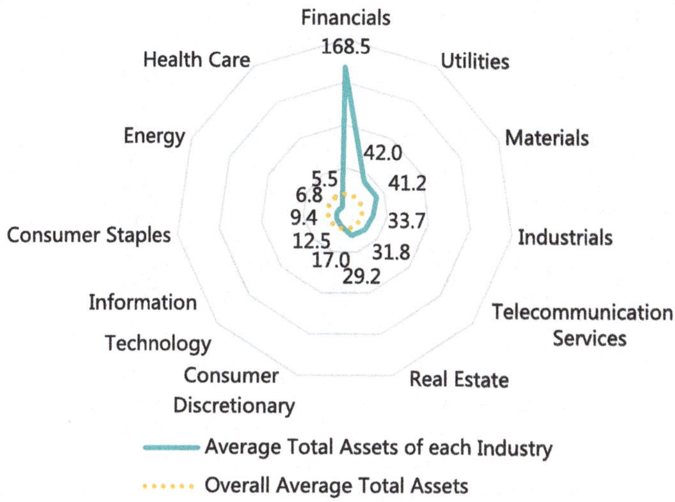


**Fig. 4.6** Average assets of ZLCs in each industry in 2017 (¥ billions)

**Table 4.1** The total assets of ZLC in Internet/non-Internet industry in 2017

| | Number of ZLC | Total assets (billion yuan) | Average total assets (billion yuan) |
|---|---|---|---|
| Non-Internet | 271 | 5580.7 | 20.6 |
| Internet | 41 | 798.3 | 19.5 |

### 4.1.4 Analysis on Assets Structure

The proportion of fixed assets refers to the ratio of fixed assets to total assets. The lower the proportion of fixed assets, the more asset-light the company is. The proportion of fixed assets of ZLCs have been kept at around 15% for five years, far lower than those of A-share, HK and U.S. listed companies. Therefore, ZLCs have relatively fewer physical assets[1] (Fig. 4.7).

[1] With data from Wind, the ratio was calculated by the editor. In order to ensure the objectivity of the results, companies in Financials and Real Estate in each capital market were excluded in the calculation.

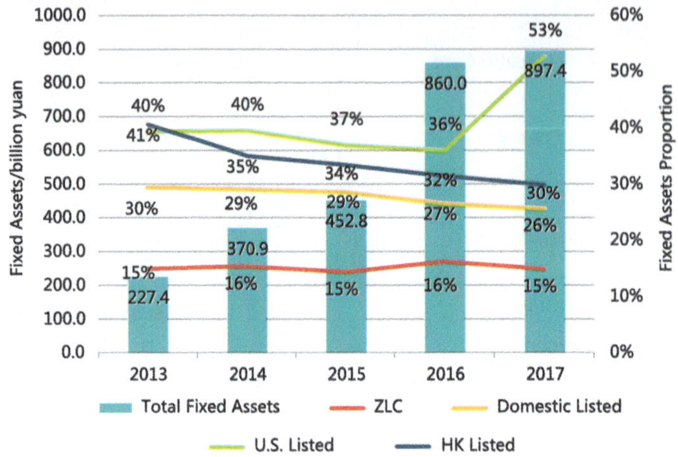


**Fig. 4.7** The comparison of fixed assets proportion between ZLCs and each capital market in 2017

## 4.2 Analysis on Debt Paying Abilities

### *4.2.1 Short-Term Debt Paying Abilities*

(1) Current Ratio

Current ratio[2] measures whether a company has enough resources to meet its short-term obligations. It compares a company's current assets to its current liabilities. Generally speaking, the higher the ratio, the stronger the short-term debt paying abilities of the company. In 2017, seven of the 312 ZLCs (2%) had a current ratio of more than 10; and 147 ZLCs (47%) had a current ratio of 2–10, which indicates better short-term debt paying abilities. There were 128 companies (41%) with a current ratio of 1–2 and 30 companies (10%) with a current ratio of less than 1. The companies with a liquidity ratio less than 1 should take precautions against possible debt risks (Fig. 4.8).

Among the seven companies with a current ratio of more than 10 in the above figure, four companies were in the Health Care industry, and the other three were in Information Technology, Materials and Energy. The top three industries by average current ratio were Health Care, Information Technology and Consumer Staples. The average current ratio of companies in these three industries were 2.59, 1.58 and 1.44, respectively. It can be seen that ZLCs in Health Care and the Information Technology have good short-term debt paying abilities. Companies in six industries, Health Care, Information Technology, Consumer Staples, Telecommunications Services, Energy

[2]Current Ratio = Current Assets/Current Liabilities.

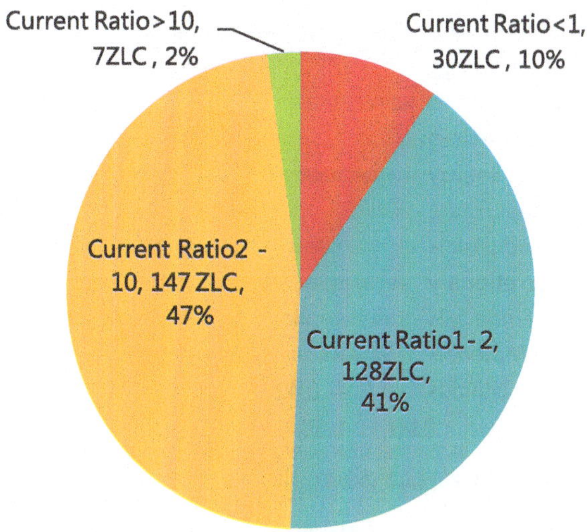


**Fig. 4.8** Current ratio of ZLCs in 2017

**Table 4.2** Current ratio of ZLCs in each industry in 2017

| Industry | Number of ZLCs | Current assets (billion yuan) | Current liabilities (billion yuan) | Average current ratio |
|---|---|---|---|---|
| Health care | 31 | 108.0 | 41.7 | 2.59 |
| Information technology | 127 | 879.6 | 555.0 | 1.58 |
| Consumer staples | 5 | 20.3 | 14.1 | 1.44 |
| Telecommunication services | 2 | 50.1 | 34.9 | 1.44 |
| Energy | 7 | 16.5 | 13.0 | 1.27 |
| Real estate | 2 | 56.1 | 45.6 | 1.23 |
| Industrials | 73 | 1619.1 | 1379.0 | 1.17 |
| Consumer discretionary | 41 | 390.1 | 339.4 | 1.15 |
| Financials | 2 | 175.4 | 173.8 | 1.01 |
| Materials | 16 | 313.4 | 338.0 | 0.93 |
| Utilities | 6 | 33.2 | 78.4 | 0.42 |
| Overall | 312 | 3662.0 | 3012.9 | 1.22 |

and Real Estate, reported higher-than-average current ratio. The average current ratio of companies in the other five industries were lower than the overall average (Table 4.2, Figs. 4.9 and 4.10).

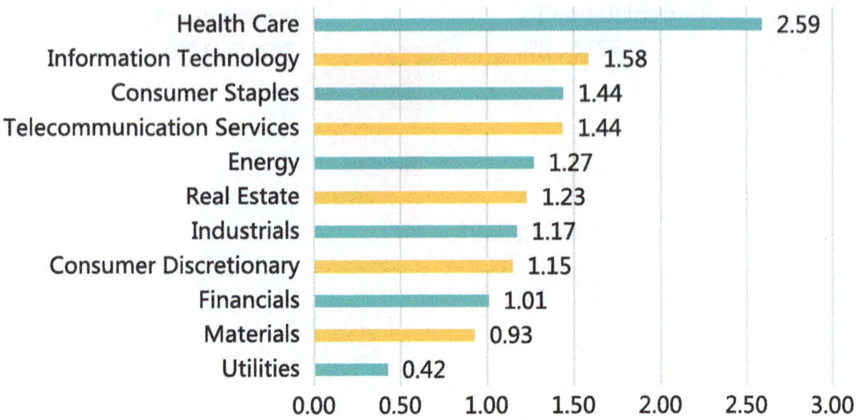


**Fig. 4.9** Current ratio of ZLCs in each industry in 2017

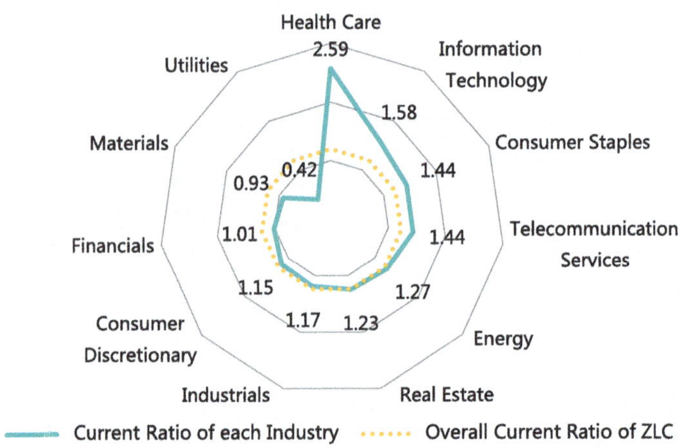


**Fig. 4.10** Current ratio of ZLCs in each industry in 2017

**Table 4.3** Current ratio of ZLCs in Internet/non-Internet industry in 2017

| | Number of ZLCs | Current assets (billion yuan) | Current liabilities (billion yuan) | Average current ratio |
|---|---|---|---|---|
| Non-Internet | 271 | 3189.2 | 2696.3 | 1.18 |
| Internet | 41 | 472.8 | 316.5 | 1.49 |

The average current ratio of ZLCs in the non-Internet industry companies was 1.18, while that of Internet companies was 1.49. In terms of short-term debt paying abilities, Internet companies were superior to non-Internet industry companies on average (Table 4.3).

(2) Quick Ratio

Quick ratio[3] compares a company's quick assets to current liabilities. It measures a company's abilities to turn its current assets into cash so as to pay current liabilities. In 2017, among 312 ZLC, six had a quick ratio of more than 10, accounting for 2%. There were 124 companies with quick ratios of 2–10, accounting for 40%. The quick ratio of 119 companies was between 1 and 2, accounting for 38%. Sixty-three companies had a quick ratio of less than 1, accounting for 20% (Fig. 4.11).

Among the six companies whose quick ratio exceeded 10, there was one Information Technology company, one Energy company, one Materials company and three Health Care companies. The average quick ratios of companies in Health Care, Information Technology and Telecommunications Services were 2.07, 1.41, and 1.34, respectively, beating the rest industries. This shows the good short-term debt paying abilities of companies in Health Care and Information Technology once again. There were five industries with an average quick ratio higher than the average quick ratio of all ZLCs, namely, Health Care, Information Technology, Telecommunications Services, Real Estate and Energy; the average quick ratios of the remaining six industries were lower than the overall average (Table 4.4, Figs. 4.12 and 4.13).

The average quick ratio of companies in the non-Internet industry was 0.89, while that of Internet companies was 1.35. The same conclusion can be made that in terms of short-term debt paying abilities, Internet companies were superior to non-Internet industry companies on average (Table 4.5).

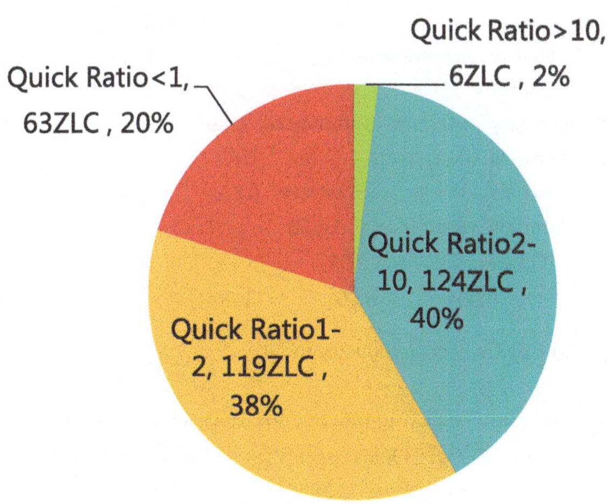


**Fig. 4.11** Quick ratio of ZLCs in 2017

[3]Quick Ratio = (Current Assets − Inventories)/Current Liabilities.

**Table 4.4** Quick ratio of ZLCs in each industry in 2017

| Industry | Number of ZLCs | Quick assets (billion yuan) | Current liabilities (billion yuan) | Quick ratio |
|---|---|---|---|---|
| Health care | 31 | 86.2 | 41.7 | 2.07 |
| Information technology | 127 | 784.0 | 555.0 | 1.41 |
| Telecommunication services | 2 | 46.8 | 34.9 | 1.34 |
| Real estate | 2 | 52.1 | 45.6 | 1.14 |
| Energy | 7 | 14.7 | 13.0 | 1.13 |
| Consumer staples | 5 | 12.7 | 14.1 | 0.90 |
| Consumer discretionary | 41 | 302.3 | 339.4 | 0.89 |
| Financials | 2 | 147.6 | 173.8 | 0.85 |
| Industrials | 73 | 1150.7 | 1379.0 | 0.83 |
| Materials | 16 | 188.9 | 338.0 | 0.56 |
| Utilities | 6 | 30.9 | 78.4 | 0.39 |
| Overall | 312 | 2816.9 | 3012.9 | 0.93 |

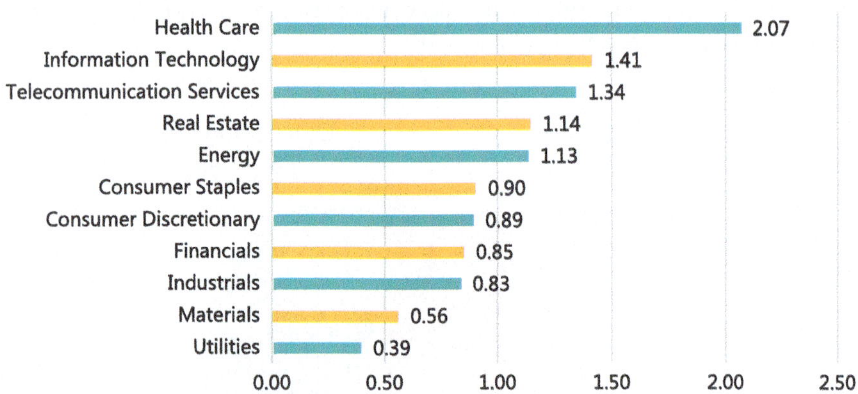


**Fig. 4.12** Quick ratio of ZLCs in each industry in 2017

**Table 4.5** Average quick ratio of ZLC in Internet/non-Internet industry in 2017

| | Number of ZLCs | Quick assets (billion yuan) | Current liabilities (billion yuan) | Average quick ratio |
|---|---|---|---|---|
| Non-Internet | 271 | 2389.1 | 2696.3 | 0.89 |
| Internet | 41 | 427.9 | 316.5 | 1.35 |

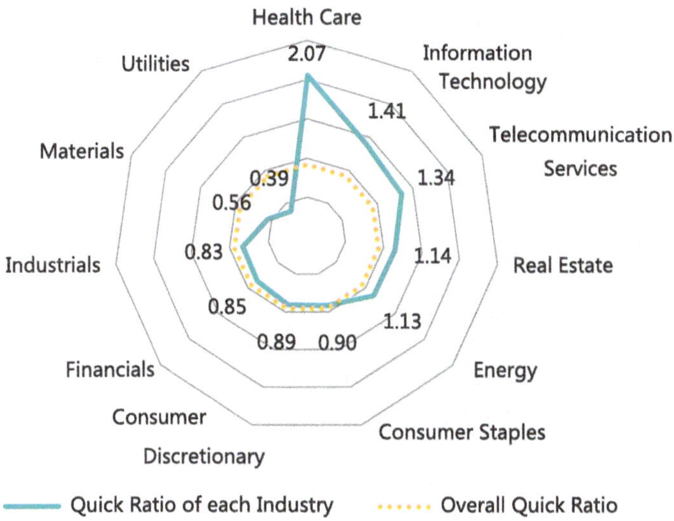


**Fig. 4.13** Quick ratio of ZLCs in each industry in 2017

### *4.2.2 Long-Term Debt Paying Abilities*

(1) Debt-to-Asset Ratio[4]

In 2017, the total liabilities of ZLC were 4039 billion yuan, and the average debt-to-asset ratio was 63.32%. The average debt-to-asset ratio of ZLCs has been kept above 60% for seven consecutive years. Among the total 312 ZLCs, 158 reported debt-to-asset ratio lower than 40%, accounting for 51%. There were 93 ZLCs with a debt-to-asset ratio of 40–60%, accounting for 30%. There are 51 ZLC with a debt-to-asset ratio of 60–80%, accounting for 16%, and 10 ZLCs with a debt-to-asset ratio higher than 80%, accounting for 3%. Even though deleveraging has been highlighted in macroeconomic regulation in recent years, the debt-to-asset ratio of ZLCs did not significantly decrease. Some companies still have overly high leverage rate and liabilities. Therefore, it is necessary to be cautious about potential risks (Fig. 4.14).

The average debt-to-asset ratios of companies in three industries, Real Estate, Financials and Industrials, were 85.07, 76.11 and 71.37%, respectively, which ranked top three. The three industries with the lowest average debt-to-asset ratios were Energy, Health Care and Consumer Staples. The average debt-to-asset ratio of companies in these three industries were 48.84, 33.29 and 33.04% respectively. The ranking on debt-to-asset ratio of different industries is consistent with the current capital structure of these industries all over China (Table 4.6, Figs. 4.15 and 4.16).

[4]Debt-to-Asset Ratio = Total Liabilities/Total Assets.

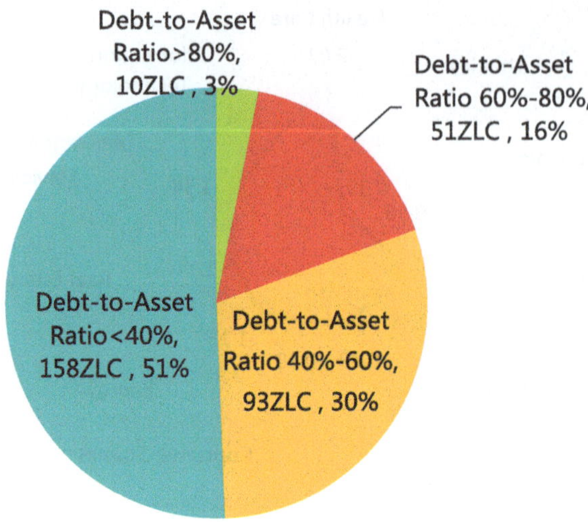


**Fig. 4.14** Debt-to-asset ratio of ZLCs in 2017

**Table 4.6** Debt-to-asset ratio of ZLCs in each industry in 2017

| Industry | Number of ZLCs | Total assets (billion yuan) | Total liabilities (billion yuan) | Debt-to-asset ratio (%) |
|---|---|---|---|---|
| Real estate | 2 | 58.4 | 49.7 | 85.07 |
| Financials | 2 | 337.0 | 256.5 | 76.11 |
| Industrials | 73 | 2458.4 | 1754.6 | 71.37 |
| Materials | 16 | 659.7 | 455.7 | 69.08 |
| Utilities | 6 | 251.8 | 170.0 | 67.51 |
| Consumer discretionary | 41 | 695.5 | 404.1 | 58.11 |
| Telecommunication services | 2 | 63.6 | 36.5 | 57.36 |
| Information technology | 127 | 1589.6 | 816.3 | 51.35 |
| Energy | 7 | 47.8 | 23.3 | 48.84 |
| Health care | 31 | 170.0 | 56.6 | 33.29 |
| Consumer staples | 5 | 47.2 | 15.6 | 33.04 |
| Overall | 312 | 6379.0 | 4039.0 | 63.32 |

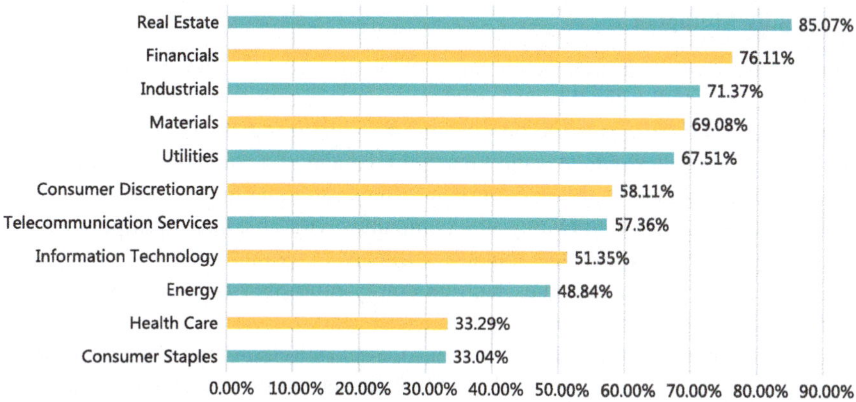


**Fig. 4.15** Debt-to-asset ratio of ZLCs in each industry in 2017

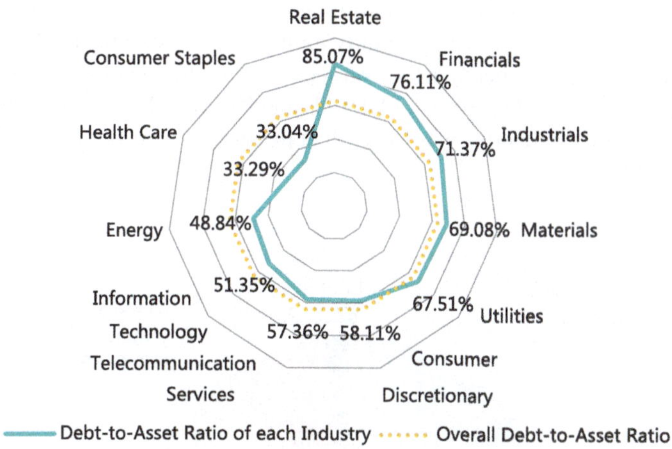


**Fig. 4.16** Debt-to-asset ratio of ZLCs in each industry in 2017

**Table 4.7** Debt-to-asset ratio of ZLCs in Internet/non-Internet industry in 2017

| | Number of ZLCs | Total assets (billion yuan) | Total liabilities (billion yuan) | Debt-to-asset ratio |
|---|---|---|---|---|
| Non-Internet | 271 | 5580.7 | 3618.5 | 0.65 |
| Internet | 41 | 798.3 | 420.5 | 0.53 |

The average debt-to-asset ratio of ZLCs in the non-Internet industry was 0.65, and that of Internet companies was 0.53 (Table 4.7).

(2) Equity Multiplier

Equity multiplier[5] measures a company's financial leverage. The greater the equity multiplier, the smaller the proportion of assets that are financed by the company's shareholders, which means the proportion of its liabilities is greater. Therefore, a high equity multiplier indicates the financial leverage of a company is big. In 2017, among the 312 ZLCs, there were six companies with an equity multiplier greater than 5, accounting for 2%; twenty-five companies with an equity multiplier of 3–5, accounting for 8%; sixty-eight companies with an equity multiplier of 2–3, accounting for 22%; and 209 companies with an equity multiplier of 1–2, accounting for 67%, which were in a majority (Fig. 4.17).

Analysis on equity multiplier and debt-to-asset ratio led to the same conclusion: companies in Real Estate, Financials and Industrials had the greatest financial leverage for their average equity multipliers were 6.70, 4.19 and 3.49, respectively; the financial leverage of companies in Energy, Health Care and Consumer Staples was the lowest, given the average equity multipliers of those companies were 1.95, 1.50 and 1.49, respectively. The average equity multipliers of Zhongguancun companies in five industries were higher than the average equity multiplier of all ZLCs. They are Real Estate, Financials, Industrials, Materials and Utilities. The financial leverage of companies in other industries was lower than the average level of ZLCs (Table 4.8, Figs. 4.18 and 4.19).

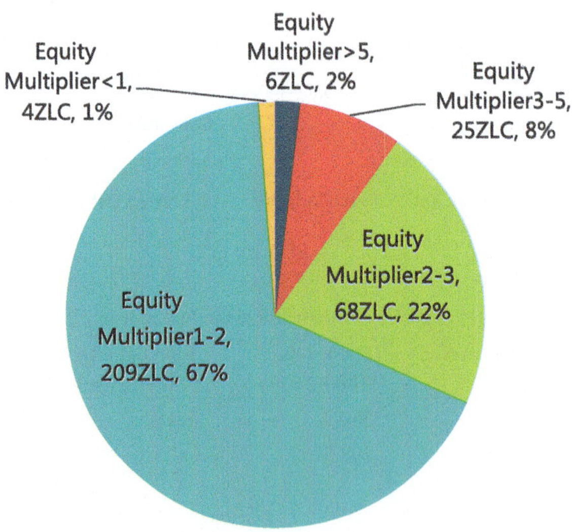


**Fig. 4.17** Equity multiplier of ZLCs in 2017

[5]Equity Multiplier = Total Assets/Total Equity.

**Table 4.8** Equity multiplier of ZLCs in each industry in 2017

| Industry | ZLC | Total assets of each industry (billion) | Equity of each industry (billion) | Equity multiplier |
|---|---|---|---|---|
| Real estate | 2 | 58.4 | 8.7 | 6.70 |
| Financials | 2 | 337.0 | 80.5 | 4.19 |
| Industrials | 73 | 2458.4 | 703.7 | 3.49 |
| Materials | 16 | 659.7 | 203.9 | 3.23 |
| Utilities | 6 | 251.8 | 81.8 | 3.08 |
| Consumer discretionary | 41 | 695.5 | 291.3 | 2.39 |
| Telecommunication services | 2 | 63.6 | 27.1 | 2.35 |
| Information technology | 127 | 1589.6 | 759.6 | 2.09 |
| Energy | 7 | 47.8 | 24.4 | 1.95 |
| Health care | 31 | 170.0 | 113.4 | 1.50 |
| Consumer staples | 5 | 47.2 | 31.6 | 1.49 |
| Overall | 312 | 6379.0 | 2326.2 | 2.74 |

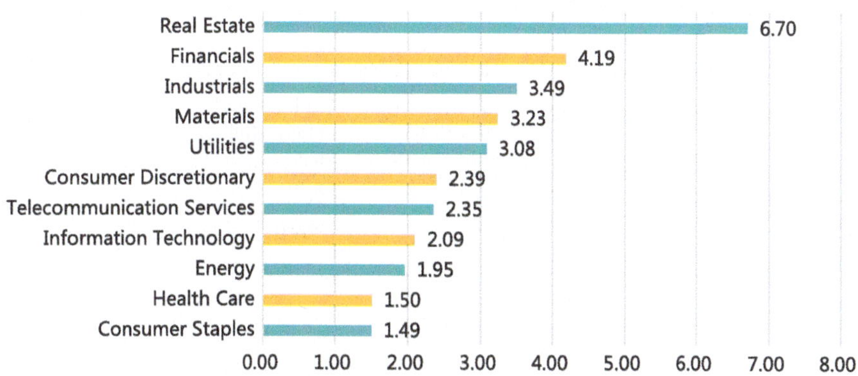


**Fig. 4.18** Equity multiplier of ZLCs in each industry in 2017

The average equity multiplier of companies in the non-Internet industry companies was 2.84, and that of Internet companies was 2.19. Among all ZLCs, the financial leverage of non-Internet companies was slightly higher than that of Internet companies (Table 4.9).

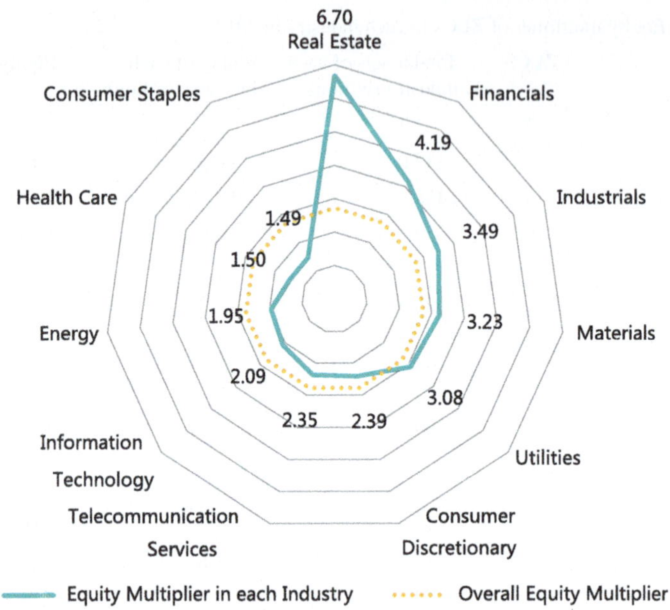


**Fig. 4.19** Equity multiplier of ZLCs in each industry in 2017

**Table 4.9** Equity multiplier of ZLCs in Internet/non-Internet industry in 2017

| | Number of ZLCs | Total assets of each industry (billion yuan) | Equity of each industry (billion yuan) | Equity multiplier |
|---|---|---|---|---|
| Non-Internet | 271 | 5580.7 | 1962.2 | 2.84 |
| Internet | 41 | 798.3 | 364.0 | 2.19 |

# Chapter 5
# Operating Capability of ZLCs in 2017

## 5.1 Analysis on Operating Capability

Operating capability refers to a company's ability to generate profits from its assets. This report analyses the operating capability of ZLCs by means of inventory turnover, receivables turnover and total assets turnover.

Inventory turnover[1] ratio reflects how much inventory is sold over a period of time, revealing whether a company is managing its stock properly. While ensuring the continuity of production and operation, a company can use the ratio to measure the efficiency of its capital utilization, which bears on its short-term debt paying abilities. The higher the inventory turnover ratio, the stronger the ability to turn inventory assets into cash. In 2017, the average inventory turnover ratio of ZLCs was 4.06, which was higher than the 2.77 of all A-shares. The average inventory turnover ratio of U.S. listed companies (11.06) was higher than that of HK listed companies (7.51) and domestic listed companies (2.91).

Receivables turnover ratio[2] refers to how many times receivables are turned into cash over a certain period of time (usually one year). It is used to measure the degree of liquidity of accounts receivable. Under general circumstances, the higher the turnover ratio of accounts receivable, the shorter the average collection period of the company. In 2017, the receivables turnover ratio of all ZLCs was 4.73, which was lower than of 9.73 of all A-shares. The receivables turnover ratio of U.S. listed companies (15.77) was higher than that of domestic listed companies (4.24) and HK listed companies (4.18).

Total asset turnover ratio[3] measures the efficiency of a company in terms of using its assets to generate revenue. The greater the total asset turnover ratio, the better

[1]Inventory turnover ratio = operating cost/annual average inventory.

[2]Receivables turnover ratio = total revenue/annual average receivables.

[3]Total asset turnover ratio = total revenue/annual total assets.



Zhongguancun Listed Companies Association, *The Competitiveness Report of Zhongguancun Listed Companies (2018)*,
https://doi.org/10.1007/978-981-13-7697-9_5

**Table 5.1** Operating capabilities of ZLCs in different capital markets in 2017

| | Inventory turnover | Receivables turnover | Total asset turnover |
|---|---|---|---|
| Domestic ZLCs | 2.91 | 4.24 | 0.61 |
| U.S. listed companies | 11.06 | 15.77 | 0.87 |
| UK listed companies | 7.51 | 4.18 | 0.68 |
| Total | 4.06 | 4.73 | 0.66 |

the company is performing. In 2017,[4] the total asset turnover ratio of ZLCs was 0.66, which was higher than that of all A shares (0.18). The total asset turnover ratio (0.87) of U.S.-listed companies was higher than those of Hong Kong-listed companies (0.68) and domestic listed companies (0.61).

Overall, the average inventory turnover ratio and total asset turnover ratio of ZLCs were higher than those of all A shares. But the receivables turnover ratio of the former was lower than the latter, which indicates ZLCs are faced with a risk in the recovery of accounts receivable. U.S. listed companies were superior to domestic listed companies and HK listed companies in terms of inventory turnover, receivables turnover and total asset turnover, displaying better operating capabilities (Table 5.1).

## 5.2 Comparison of Operating Capabilities of ZLCs in Different Industries

The inventory turnover ratios of ZLCs in Utilities, Finance and Telecommunications Services were 11.72, 11.05 and 8.00 respectively, ranking top three among all Zhongguancun companies. The top three by receivables turnover ratio were companies in Consumer Staples, Consumer Discretionary, Real Estate, which were 16.56, 16.22 and 8.82 respectively, while the top three total asset turnover ratios were in Consumer Discretionary, Financial and Consumer Staples, which were 1.13, 0.96 and 0.81.

The inventory turnover, receivables turnover and total asset turnover of ZLCs in Finance and Consumer Discretionary were higher than the average level, and the overall operating capabilities of these companies were better. The inventory turnover, receivables turnover of IT companies were above average, but their total asset turnover was slightly lower than the average. For companies in Health Care, their accounts receivable turnover and total asset turnover were above average, but their inventory turnover ratio was slightly below average. The receivables turnover and total asset turnover of Consumer Staples companies were above average.

In terms of inventory turnover Utilities, companies in Finance, Telecommunications Services, Consumer Discretionary, Information Technology, Energy, and Real Estate beat the average of all ZLCs, which was 4.06 (Figs. 5.1, 5.2, 5.3 and Table 5.2).

[4]In 2017, the overall inventory turnover ratio, accounts receivable turnover ratio and total asset turnover ratio of A shares were 2.77, 9.73 and 0.18, respectively.

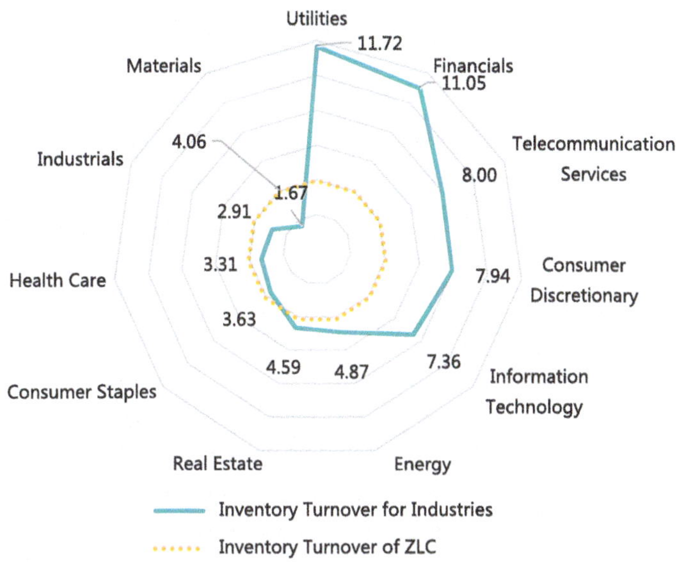


**Fig. 5.1** Inventory turnover ratio of ZLCs in different industries in 2017

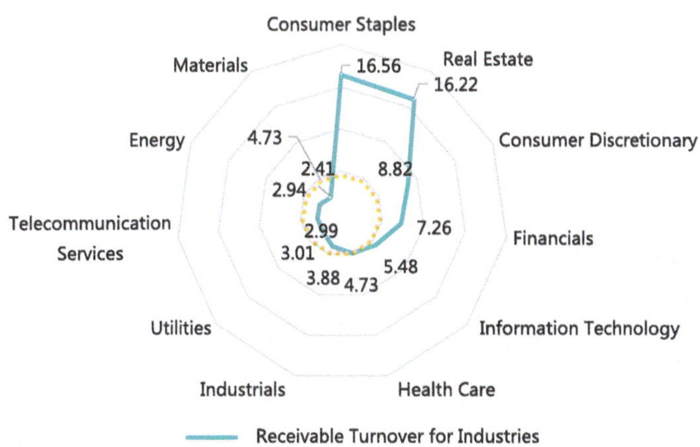


**Fig. 5.2** Receivable turnover ratio of ZLCs in different industries in 2017

The inventory turnover ratio and receivables turnover ratio of Internet companies were far higher than those of Non-Internet industries, since the former have less inventory and can collect receivables more quickly. Besides, the total asset turnover ratio of Internet companies is also slightly higher than that of Non-Internet companies. To conclude, ZLCs in the Internet industry are superior to Non-Internet companies in terms of overall operating capabilities (Table 5.3).

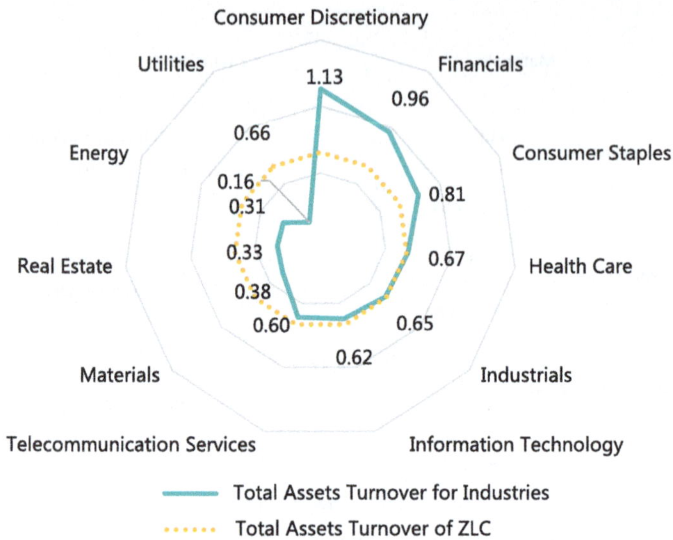


**Fig. 5.3** Total assets turnover ratio of ZLCs in different industries in 2017

**Table 5.2** Comparison of operation capabilities of ZLCs in various industries in 2017

| Industry | Inventory turnover | Receivables turnover | Total asset turnover |
|---|---|---|---|
| Utilities | 11.72 | 3.01 | 0.16 |
| Finance | 11.05 | 7.26 | 0.96 |
| Telecommunication services | 8.00 | 2.99 | 0.60 |
| Consumer discretionary | 7.94 | 8.82 | 1.13 |
| Information technology | 7.36 | 5.48 | 0.62 |
| Energies | 4.87 | 2.94 | 0.31 |
| Real estate | 4.59 | 16.22 | 0.33 |
| Consumer staples | 3.63 | 16.56 | 0.81 |
| Health care | 3.31 | 4.73 | 0.67 |
| Industries | 2.91 | 3.88 | 0.65 |
| Materials | 1.67 | 2.41 | 0.38 |
| Overall average | 4.06 | 4.73 | 0.66 |

**Table 5.3** Operating capabilities of ZLC' internet/non-internet industries in 2017

| | Inventory turnover | Receivable turnover | Total asset turnover |
|---|---|---|---|
| Internet | 11.56 | 11.23 | 0.85 |
| Non-Internet | 3.67 | 4.28 | 0.63 |

# Chapter 6
# Innovation Capabilities of ZLCs in 2017

## 6.1 Innovation Input

### *6.1.1 R&D Investment of ZLCs*

Research and development activities are an important source of innovation, and innovation is the key to maintain a company's core competitiveness. Only by increasing investment in innovative activities can companies enhance their competitiveness and ensure long-term development. Numerous studies have shown that although R&D expenditures may hurt cash flow in a short run, but in a longer term have a positive impact on financial performance, which includes profitability and market value.

Based on international research and general business development, an enterprise can survive when its R&D intensity (R&D costs as a proportion of revenue) reaches at 2% and will thrive competitively when R&D intensity reaches 5%. In this report, we have selected ten leading, global innovative high-tech companies, including Apple, Google, Cisco, Facebook, Intel, HP, NVIDIA, Oracle, eBay and Huawei. We calculated the average R&D intensity of these ten companies in 2017. Based on our analysis, the average R&D intensity of these companies was 11.34%, which indicates that 10% R&D intensity is the average level amongst high-level, global high-tech companies.

A total of 281 ZLCs disclosed annual R&D data in 2017, accounting for 90.06% of the total. The total research and development expenses of these companies reached 122 billion yuan, increasing 18% y-o-y, and the average R&D intensity was 3.31%, increasing by 12% y-o-y. The average R&D intensity of ZLCs was higher than that of A-share companies (1.48%) (Fig. 6.1).

Among the 281 ZLCs, 78 companies reported an R&D intensity of over 10%, accounting for 28%, 73 companies of 5–10%, accounting for 26%, 83 companies of 2–5%, accounting for 30%, and 46 companies of below 2%, accounting for 16%.[1]

[1] As SEED.O did not disclose its revenue, its R&D intensity could not be calculated.



Zhongguancun Listed Companies Association, *The Competitiveness Report of Zhongguancun Listed Companies (2018)*,
https://doi.org/10.1007/978-981-13-7697-9_6

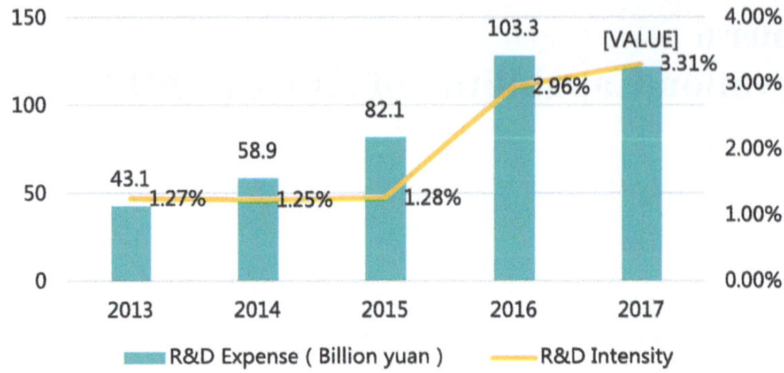


**Fig. 6.1** R&D investment of ZLCs in 2013–2017

**Fig. 6.2** R&D intensity distribution among ZLCs in 2017

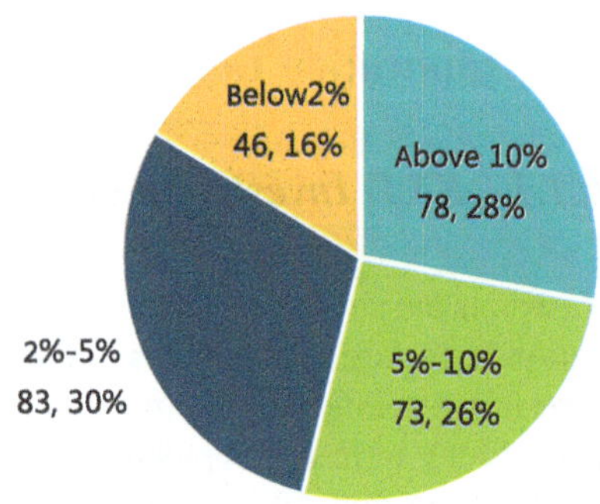


It can be seen that the R&D investment of ZLCs is quite high as a whole, and that the R&D input of nearly 30% of ZLCs has reached a high level worldwide (Fig. 6.2).

### *6.1.2 Rankings of R&D Expenditures and R&D Intensity*

The top 30 ZLCs by R&D expenditures spent nearly 90.9 billion yuan on research and development activities in 2017. The money accounted for 75% of the total R&D expenses of ZLCs. There were two companies with R&D expenditures of over 10 billion, namely Baidu (12.928 billion yuan) and China Railway Group (120.20 billion yuan). Among the top 30 companies, 20 were in Information Technology Industry, five in Industrials, three in Consumer Discretionary, and the rest two were in Telecommunications Services and Health Care. Ten were Internet companies, namely Baidu, Jingdong, Sohu, Sina, 58.com, Weibo, Sogou, LeTV, Autohome, Changyou, while the remaining 20 were Non-Internet companies.

In 2017, the R&D intensity of all ZLCs on the top 30 R&D intensity ranking all exceeded 19%, ranging from 20 to 30%. There were eight companies whose R&D intensity exceeded 30%. They were BeiGene (112.85),[2] China Binary (42.95%), Lianluo hey were (39.07%), Xinwei (35.44%), Sevenstar (33.13%), Sinovel (31.00%), Ingenic (30.76%).

From the perspective of industry distribution, according to Wind Primary Industry Classification Standard, the top 30 companies with R&D intensity were mainly concentrated in the Information Technology (22), and the rest were scattered in Health Care (2), Industrial (2), Consumer Discretionary (1), Energy (1), Telecommunications Services (1) and Materials (1). According to the criteria of Internet and Non-Internet industry classification, there were 8 top 30 Internet companies in 2017, namely China Binery, Linekong, Ourpalm, NSFOCUS, Changyou, SOHU.COM, Sogou, and the remaining 22 belonged to Non-Internet companies.

Comparing the two rankings of R&D expense ranking and R&D intensity ranking, it could be seen that companies with high R&D expenses and R&D intensity were mainly concentrated in the Information Technology, which was closely related to the characteristics of its high technical requirements. In addition, all of the 9 listed companies, BeiGene, Sinovel, Sevenstar, KingSoft, Changyou, SOHU.COM, ChinaSoft, YONYOU, Sougo, were listed in both of the top 30 rankings of R&D Investment and R&D intensity (Figs. 6.3, 6.4).

### *6.1.3 The Industry Distribution of R&D Expense and R&D Intensity*

In 2017, companies in Information Technology, Industrial and Consumer Discretionary accounted for an overwhelming majority of the total R&D expenses of all ZLCs. They spent 66.9 billion yuan, 32.6 billion yuan and 13.8 billion yuan respectively on R&D activities. The total R&D expenses of these three industries was 113.3 billion yuan, accounting for 93% of the total. The average R&D expenses of the four industries—Telecommunication Services, Information Technology, Consumer Discretionary and Industrials—were higher than the overall average R&D expenses of ZLCs (434 million yuan). In addition, the average R&D intensity of the three major industries of Information Technology, Health Care, and Telecommunications Services was 7.50, 4.33, and 3.80%, which were all higher than the overall average R&D intensity (3.31%). The main reason is that the three industries all have higher requirements for technical patents (Figs. 6.5, 6.6, Table 6.1).

The average R&D expenses and R&D intensity of ZLCs in the Internet industry were higher than those of Non-Internet companies (Table 6.2).

[2]BGNE.O is a global, commercial, research-based biotechnology company focused on the development and commercialization of molecular targeting and immunotherapy. The increase in the company's R&D expenses in 2017 was on account of the increase in expenditures from the progress of clinical trials to the later stages, the increase in the production expenditure of drug candidates was because of the expansion of clinical projects in progress, and the employee compensation was on account of the increase in the number of people supporting the company's clinical programs.

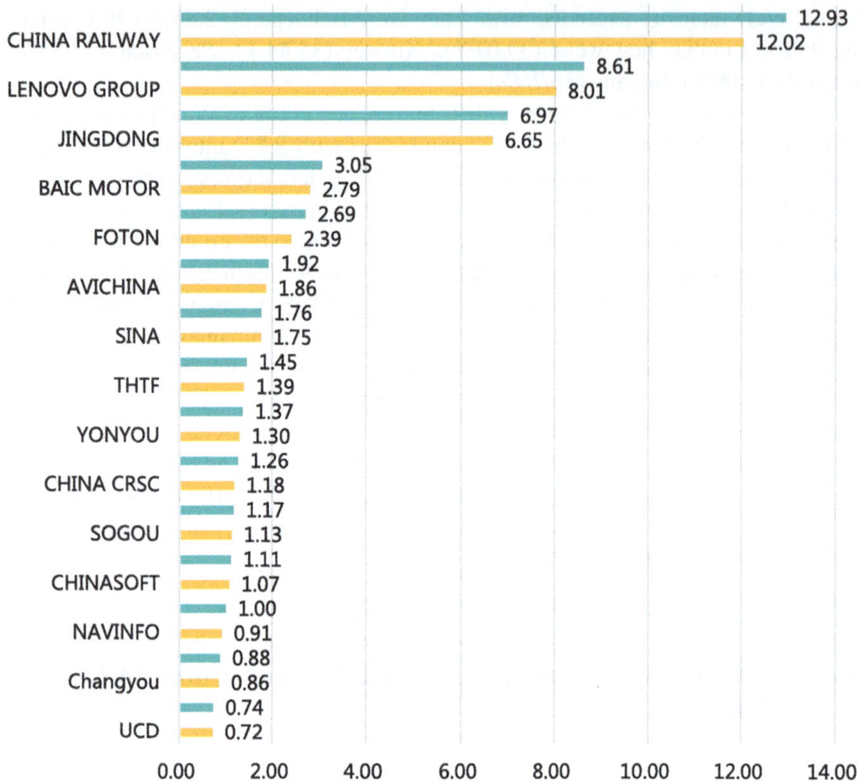


**Fig. 6.3** Top 30 ZLCs by R&D expenses in 2017 (Billion yuan)

### *6.1.4 Relationship Between R&D Input and Profitability*

According to Fig. 6.7, for five consecutive years from 2013 to 2017, companies whose R&D intensity was lower than 2% reported a lower gross profit on a whole, while those with a R&D intensity of over 10% were superior to the rest in terms of gross profit. It is thus concluded that a company's gross profit is positively correlated with its R&D intensity as long as the intensity is within a reasonable range. Therefore, reasonable R&D investment can help promote profitability. Companies should increase R&D input according to their own scale and capacity to maximize the benefits of innovation.

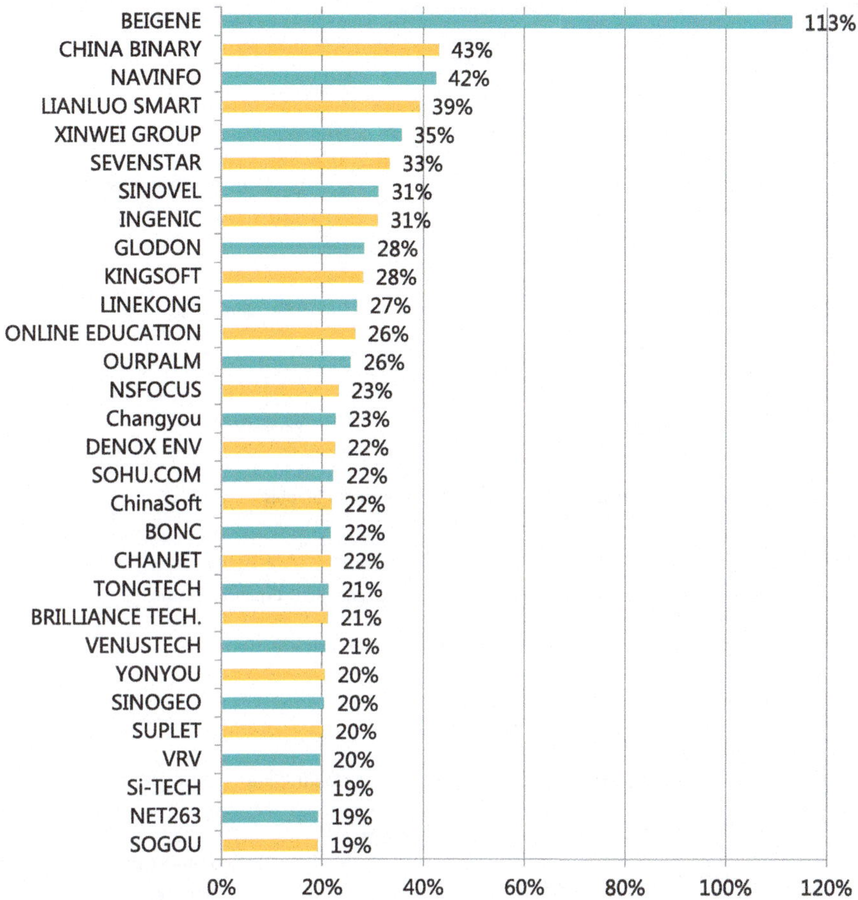


**Fig. 6.4** Top 30 ZLCs by R&D intensity in 2017

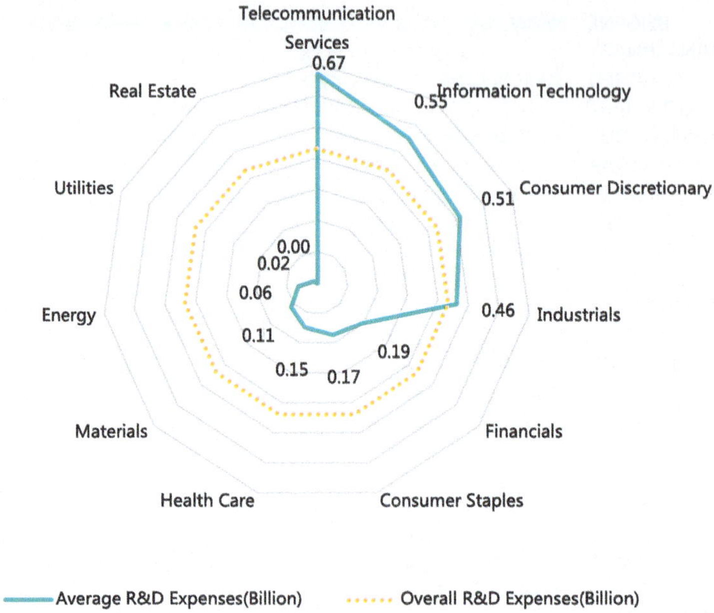


**Fig. 6.5** Average R&D expenses of ZLCs in different industries in 2017

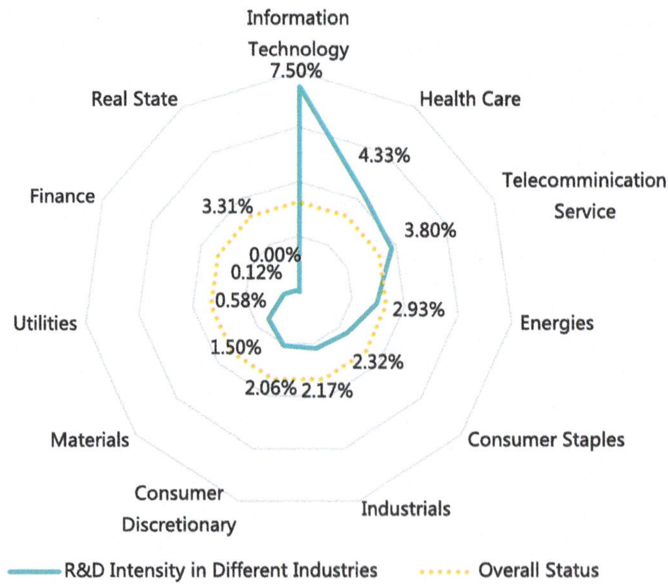


**Fig. 6.6** Average R&D intensity of ZLCs across industries in 2017

**Table 6.1** R&D expenses and R&D intensity across industries in 2017

| Industry | R&D expenses (Billion yuan) | Number of ZLCs | Average R&D expenses (Billion yuan) | R&D intensity (%) |
|---|---|---|---|---|
| Information technology | 66.80 | 121 | 0.55 | 7.50 |
| Health care | 3.97 | 27 | 0.15 | 4.33 |
| Telecommunication service | 1.34 | 2 | 0.67 | 3.80 |
| Energy | 0.38 | 6 | 0.06 | 2.93 |
| Consumer staples | 0.86 | 5 | 0.17 | 2.32 |
| Industrials | 32.60 | 71 | 0.46 | 2.17 |
| Consumer discretionary | 13.82 | 27 | 0.51 | 2.06 |
| Materials | 1.71 | 15 | 0.11 | 1.50 |
| Utilities | 0.08 | 5 | 0.02 | 0.58 |
| Finance | 0.39 | 2 | 0.19 | 0.12 |
| Real state | 0.00 | 0 | 0.00 | 0.00 |
| Overall | 122.03 | 281 | 0.43 | 3.31 |

**Table 6.2** R&D input of internet/non-internet industries in 2017

| | Average R&D expense (Billion yuan) | R&D expense (Billion yuan) | R&D intensity (%) |
|---|---|---|---|
| Non-internet | 0.4 | 86.7 | 2.79 |
| Internet | 1 | 35.4 | 6.04 |

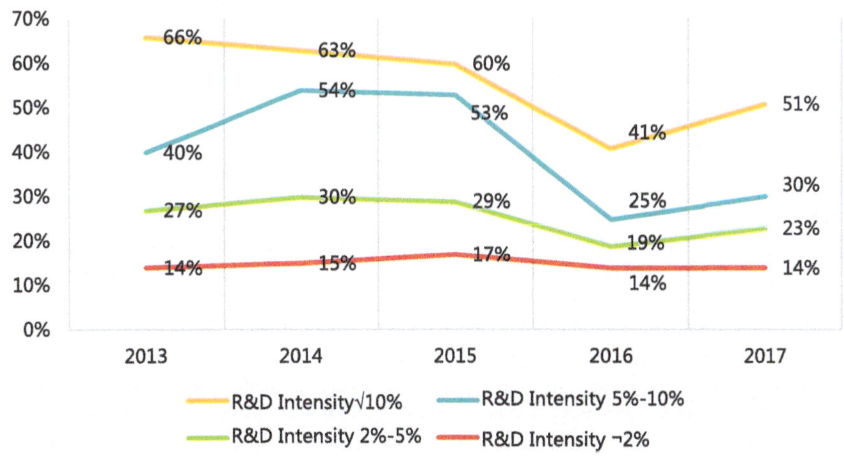


**Fig. 6.7** Relationship between R&D intensity and gross profit of ZLCs in 2013–2017

## 6.2 Innovation Output[3]

### *6.2.1 Patent Application and Ranking*[4]

Patent application volume refers to the number of patents that have been accepted by patent organisations, including invention patents,[5] utility model patents[6] and design patents.[7] Among the three categories of patent, invention patents have the longest term of protection and require the longest time to obtain regulatory approval. The greater patent application of a company, the stronger its innovation capabilities.

In 2017, 63% of domestic listed Zhongguancun companies (138 companies) filed 8857 patent applications, up 4% y-o-y. On average, every company filed 64.18 patent applications. There were 13 companies whose patent application volume was above the average. To be more specific, 6705 invention patents were applied by 123 companies, accounting for 75.70% of the total, up 12% y-o-y, with each company applying for 54.51 on average. The above mentioned data indicated that domestic listed Zhongguancun companies have been increasingly keen on seeking patent protection (see Fig. 6.8).

On the 2017 ranking of patent application volume, the top 10 domestic listed Zhongguancun companies filed 6776 patent applications, taking up 76.50% of the total. The ten companies were BOE-B, FOTON, Aisino Corporation, Bnbmplc, Tianli, Si-Tech, Gigadevice, Wanji Tech, BGE, iReader Technology. Among them, the patent application volume of BOE-B was 4968, accounting for 73.32% of the total, far more than that of FOTON, Aisino Corporation, and the rest. Patent application volume sees highly concentrated distribution in Zhongguancun, which indicates that a few of ZLCs have exceptional R&D capabilities. These companies not only lead the whole industry but also promote the overall R&D level of Zhongguancun (see Fig. 6.9).

[3]The data source of this part is the Zhongguancun Intellectual Property Promotion Bureau. To ensure the accessibility and accuracy of data, only the patent data of domestic listed Zhongguancun companies is analysed in this report.

[4]A company's patent application refers to the amount of patent applications filed by the company in the current year, including invention patent, utility model patent and design patent.

[5]Invention patent may be granted for novel, creative and practical methods and products. It has the highest technical requirement and commercial value. Its term of protection is 20 years.

[6]Utility model patent may be granted in China for technical solutions that relate to shapes or structures, and has a term of 10 years from the date of filing.

[7]Design patent is granted to any person who has invented any new, original and ornamental design for an article of manufacture, and has a term of 10 years from the date of filing.

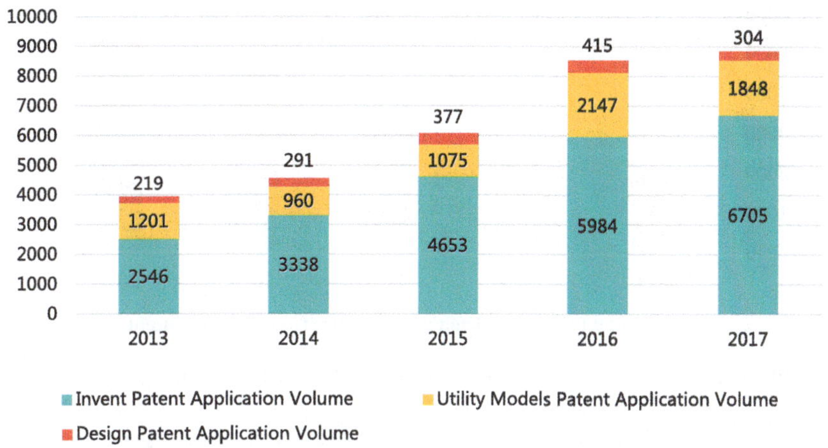


**Fig. 6.8** Patent application volume of domestic listed companies in Zhongguancun in 2013–2017

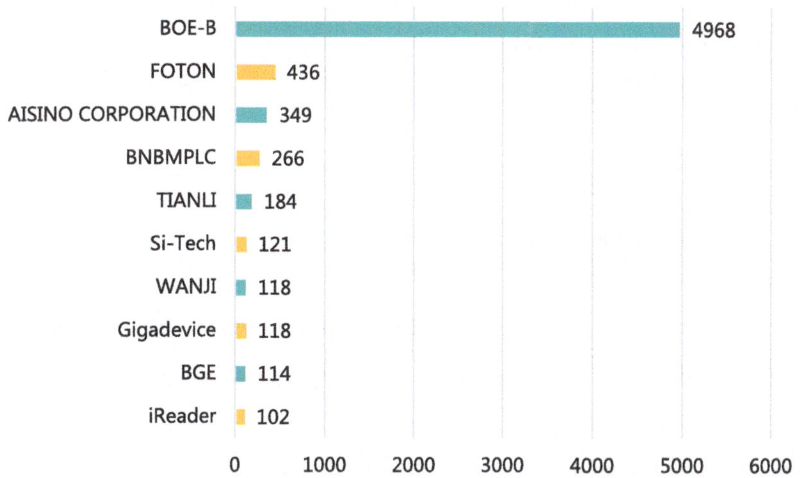


**Fig. 6.9** Top 10 domestic listed Zhongguancun companies by patent application volume in 2017

### *6.2.2 Number of Patents and Ranking*[8]

Number of patents is an important indicator to measure a company's innovation capabilities. In 2017, 149 Zhongguancun domestic listed companies obtained 5435 patents, increasing by 15% y-o-y. On average, each company got 36.48 patents, and the number of patents of 17 ZLCs beat the average. There were 121 companies obtaining 3480 invention patents, which accounted for 64.03% of the total patents

[8]Number of patents refers to the amount of patents for invention, utility model and design granted by patent administrations.

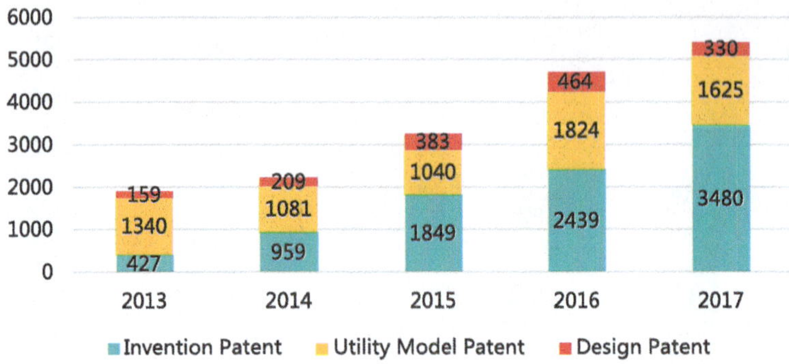


**Fig. 6.10** Number of patents granted to domestic listed Zhongguancun companies in 2013–2017

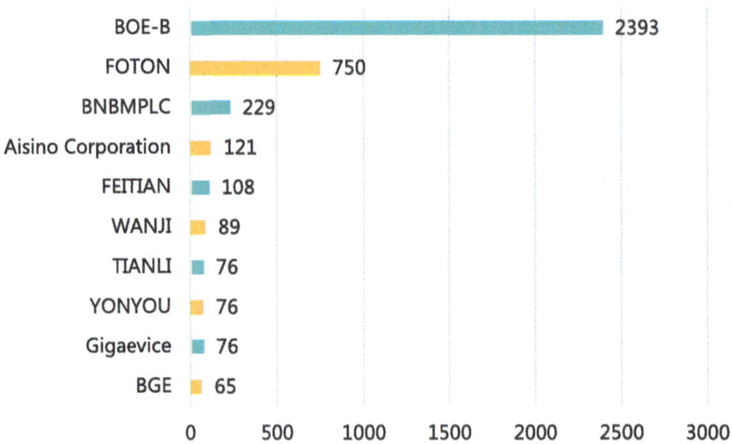


**Fig. 6.11** Top 10 domestic listed Zhongguancun companies by number of patents

granted to all ZLCs, up 43% y-o-y. Each of them got 28.76 invention patents averagely. Data show that the growth rate of patents granted to Zhongguancun domestic listed companies has slowed down, indicating that the R&D capabilities of these companies have reached a rather high level and will continue to rise (see Fig. 6.10).

In 2017, the top ten domestic listed Zhongguancun companies by number of patents obtained a total of 3983 patents, accounting for 73.28% of the total number of applications in the year. The ten companies were BOE-B, Foton, Bnbmplc, Aisino Corporation, Feitian, Wanji, Gigadevice, Yonyou, Tianli, and BGE. Among them, the number of patents of BOE was 2393, far more than those of the others (see Figs. 6.11, 6.12).

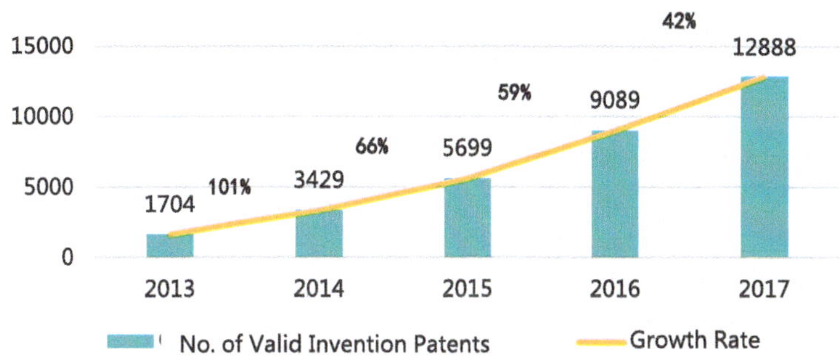


**Fig. 6.12** Number of valid invention patents of domestic listed Zhongguancun companies in 2013–2017

### 6.2.3 Number of Valid Invention Patents and Ranking[9]

As of December 31, 2017, a total of 165 domestic listed Zhongguancun companies had obtained 12,888 valid invention patents, up 42% y-o-y. On average, each company own 78.11 valid invention patents. In 2017, the number of valid invention patents held by domestic listed Zhongguancun companies grew over the previous year, and the value of innovation output continued to rise.

The top ten domestic listed companies in Zhongguancun by number of valid invention patents obtained 9039 valid invention patents, accounting for 70.14% of the total valid invention patents in the current year. They were BOE-B, Foton, Feitian, Hanvon, Sifang, Yonyou, Aisino corporation, AT&M, Gigadevice, and SJEP. BOE-B far surpassed other listed companies not only in terms of patent applications and number of patents. The number of valid invention patents of the company was 5810, which was much higher than the others and accounted for 45% of the total (Fig. 6.13).

### 6.2.4 PCT Patent Application

PCT (the abbreviation of the Patent Cooperation Treaty)[10] is an international cooperation treaty in the field of intellectual property. It aims to enable intellectual property owners to obtain intellectual property protection in a more economical manner. The

[9]Valid invention patents refer to invention patents within the term, including the invention patents granted in 2017, those maintained valid with annual fees paid and the invention patents owned by newly listed companies.

[10]The Patent Cooperation Treaty provides a unified procedure for filing patent applications to protect inventions in each of its contracting states. Applicants only need to file an application in one language to seek patent protection for an invention simultaneously in each of the contracting countries. Therefore, filing an application under the PCT is simpler, easier and more cost-effective.

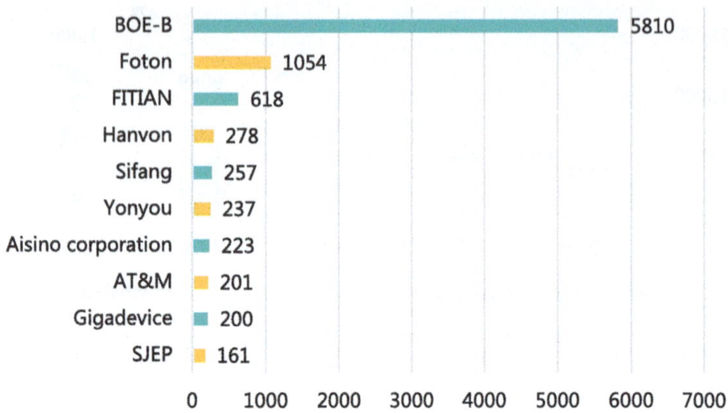


**Fig. 6.13** Top 10 domestic listed companies in Zhongguancun by number of valid invention patents in 2017

PCT makes it possible to seek patent protection for an invention simultaneously in a large number of countries.

In 2017, 16 Zhongguancun domestic listed companies filed PCT applications, which totalled 1695, up 5% y-o-y. The number of PCT applications of domestic listed companies in Zhongguancun has been growing steadily. BOE-B filed 1649 PTC applications, accounting for 97% of the total. It's worth noting that the number of PTC applications filed by the other companies was quite low, which indicates their insufficient efforts to seek patent protection for their inventions outside China (Fig. 6.14).

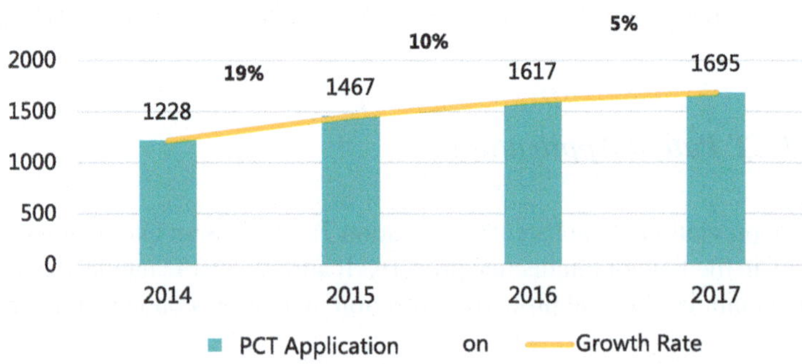


**Fig. 6.14** Number of PCT application of domestic listed companies in Zhongguancun in 2014–2017

**Table 6.3** Industry distribution of ZLCs' patents in 2017

| Industry | Patent application | | Patent | | Valid patent for invention | | PCT application | |
|---|---|---|---|---|---|---|---|---|
| | Number of companies | Number of patent applications | Number of companies | Number of patents | Number of companies | Number of valid patent for invention | Number of companies | Number of PCT applications |
| Information technology | 59 | 6770 | 63 | 3445 | 70 | 9243 | 8 | 1669 |
| Industrials | 48 | 1031 | 49 | 715 | 53 | 1426 | 3 | 4 |
| Consumer discretionary | 6 | 588 | 7 | 810 | 7 | 1076 | 2 | 13 |
| Materials | 9 | 367 | 10 | 340 | 10 | 619 | 2 | 5 |
| Health care | 8 | 66 | 10 | 33 | 13 | 283 | 0 | 0 |
| Consumer staples | 4 | 14 | 4 | 46 | 4 | 208 | 1 | 4 |
| Energy | 2 | 14 | 3 | 37 | 4 | 24 | 0 | 0 |
| Utilities | 2 | 7 | 3 | 9 | 3 | 8 | 0 | 0 |
| Telecommunication service | 0 | 0 | 0 | 0 | 1 | 1 | 0 | 0 |
| Total | 138 | 8857 | 149 | 5435 | 165 | 12888 | 16 | 1695 |

### 6.2.5 *Industry Distribution of Patent*

In 2017, a vast majority of patents of ZLCs were owned by companies in three industries—Information Technology, Industrials and Consumer Discretionary. To be more specific, the three industries accounted for 95% of patent applications, 91% of patents, 91% of valid invention patents and 99% of PCT applications.

The sector of Information Technology ranked first by number of patent applications, number of patents, number of valid patents for invention and number of PCT applications. For one reason, IT companies are the largest group in Zhongguancun, and they have higher requirements for R&D. For another, most of patents in Zhongguancun are owned by BOE-B, an IT company. Its patent applications take up 56% of the total, its patents 44%, its valid patents for invention 45% and its PCT applications 97% (Table 6.3).

# Chapter 7
# Investment, Financing and Cash Position of ZLCs in 2017

## 7.1 Analysis of Cash and Cash Equivalents at the End of Term

In 2017, the balance of cash and cash equivalents at the end of term of ZLCs was 874.6 billion yuan, an increase of 6% y-o-y which was significantly lower than those of other years. There might be two reasons for the slow growth of cash and cash equivalents. Firstly, the accumulation of cash and cash equivalents of ZLCs has formed a certain scale. Secondly, due to the deleveraging in macro-economy and financial markets, financing channels for companies have been narrowed in 2017. As a result, many ZLCs were relatively short of capital (see Fig. 7.1).

From the perspective of distribution of capital markets, cash and cash equivalents of domestic listed companies accounted for the largest proportion of the ZLCs' total,

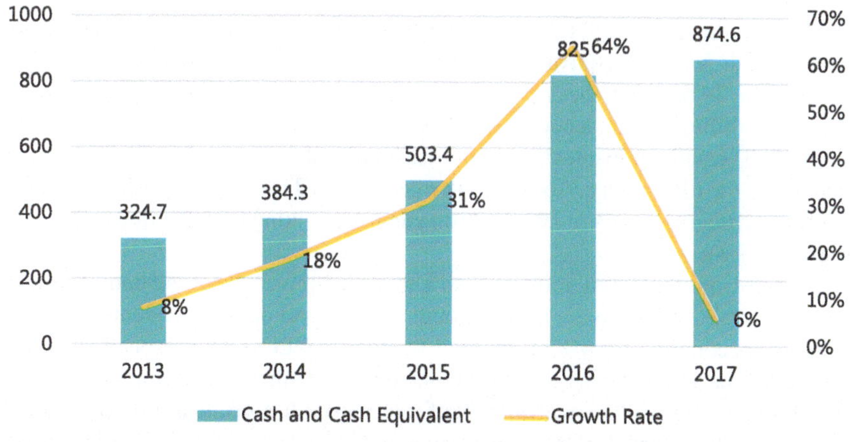


Fig. 7.1 Changes of cash and cash equivalents of ZLCs in 2013–2017 (¥ billions)


Zhongguancun Listed Companies Association, *The Competitiveness Report of Zhongguancun Listed Companies (2018)*,
https://doi.org/10.1007/978-981-13-7697-9_7

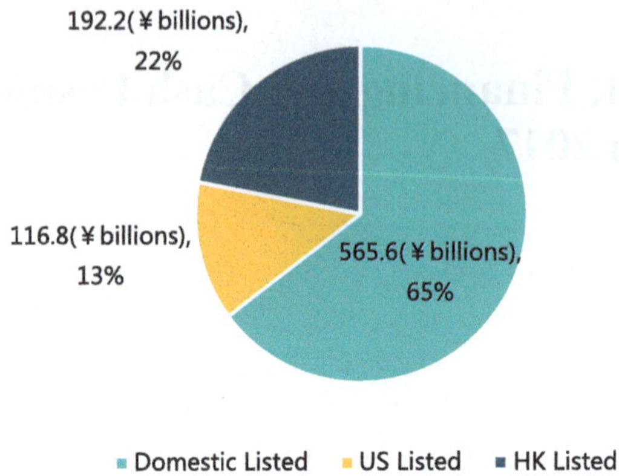


**Fig. 7.2** Distribution of cash and cash equivalents at each capital market in 2017 (¥ billions)

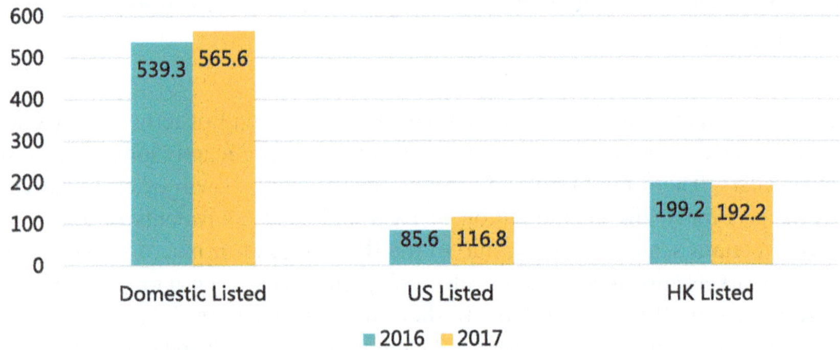


**Fig. 7.3** Changes of cash and cash equivalents of ZLCs in 2016–2017 (¥ billions)

which was more than a half. HK listed companies and U.S. listed companies followed the list. Cash and cash equivalents of U.S. companies posted the biggest year-on-year growth. To be exact, the cash and cash equivalents of domestic listed companies were 565.6 billion yuan, accounting for 65% of the total, with a y-o-y growth rate of 5%. U.S. listed companies' cash and cash equivalents were 116.8 billion yuan, accounting for 13%, with a y-o-y growth rate of 36%. The cash and cash equivalents of HK listed companies were 192.2 billion yuan, accounting for 22%, down 4% y-o-y (Figs. 7.2, 7.3).

Judging from the distribution of cash and cash equivalents at the end of term, a few large-scale ZLCs have a huge amount of cash and cash equivalents. In 2017, 14 ZLCs (accounting for 4% of the total number of ZLCs) held respectively more than 10 billion yuan of cash and cash equivalents, worth 488.1 billion yuan totally (accounting for 56% of the total amount of cash and cash equivalents). There were 15 ZLCs (accounting for 5% of the total number of ZLCs) with cash and cash equivalents between 5 and 10 billion yuan, worth 113.1 billion yuan totally (accounting for 13% of the total amount of cash and cash equivalents). There were 38 ZLCs with cash and

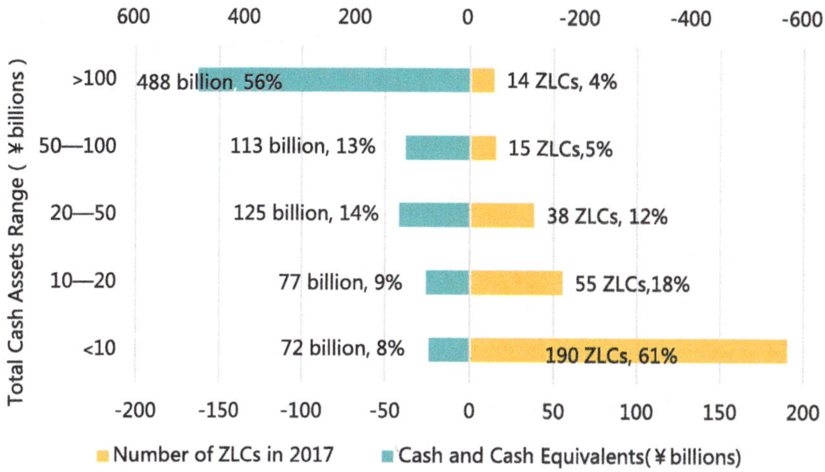


**Fig. 7.4** Distribution of cash and cash equivalents of ZLCs in 2017

cash equivalents in the range of 2–5 billion yuan (accounting for 12% of the total number of ZLCs), worth 124.6 billion yuan totally (accounting for 14% of the total amount of cash and cash equivalents). There were 55 ZLCs (18% of the total number of ZLCs) with cash and cash equivalents between 1 and 2 billion yuan, worth 76.9 billion yuan totally (9% of the total amount of cash and cash equivalents). There were 190 ZLCs (61% of the total number of ZLCs) with cash and cash equivalents less than 1 billion yuan, worth 71.9 billion yuan totally (8% of the total amount of cash and cash equivalents) (Fig. 7.4).

From the perspective of industries, according to Wind Standard Industrial Classification, the average balance of cash and cash equivalents at the end of term of five industries (finance, telecommunications industry, industrials, real estate, consumer discretionary) was above the overall average (2.8 billion yuan). That number in sectors as materials, information technology, consumer staples, utilities, health care, and energy was lower than the average. According to the standard industrial classification of Internet/non-Internet, the average balance of cash and cash equivalents at the end of term in Internet and non-Internet sectors was the same as the average, both of which were 2.8 billion yuan, showing no obvious industry characteristics (Fig. 7.5).

## 7.2 Analysis of Cash Flow Changes

In 2017, the cash flow from operating activities of ZLCs was 280.4 billion yuan, with the growth rate (only 1% y-o-y) much lower than that of 2016. The cash flow from investing activities was 457.3 billion yuan, up 12% y-o-y, indicating that ZLCs increased the investment in 2017, but the growth rate was far lower than that of 2016.

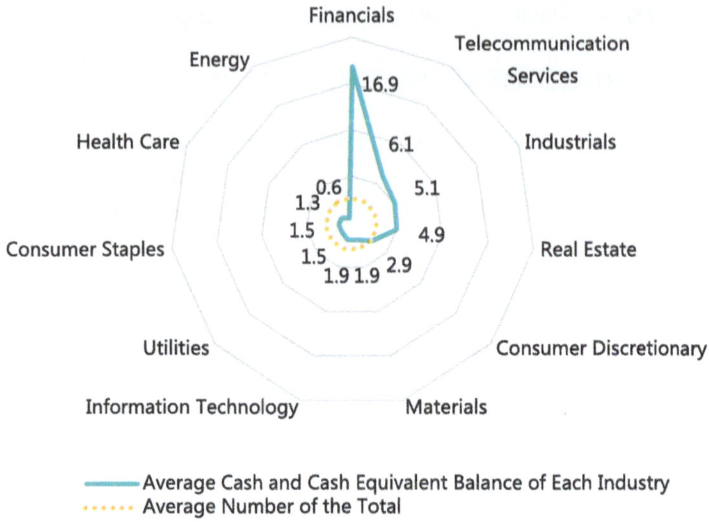


**Fig. 7.5** Average cash and cash equivalent balance of each industry in 2017 (unit: ¥ billions)

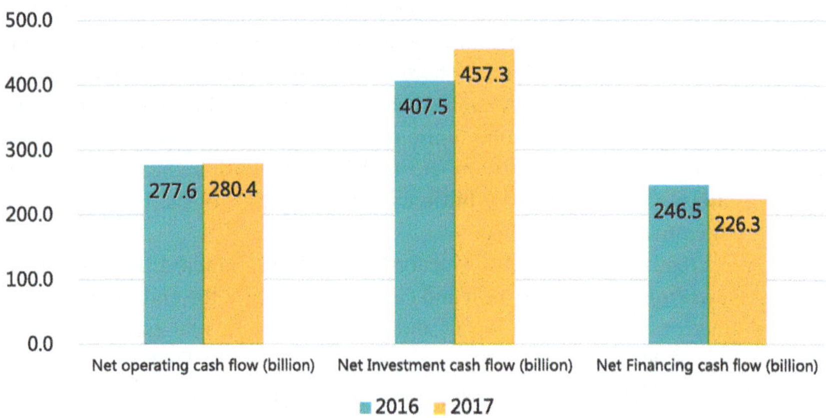


**Fig. 7.6** Changes of net operating, investment and financing cash flow of ZLCs in 2016–2017 (¥ billions)

The cash flow from financing activities was 226.3 billion yuan, down 8% y-o-y (Fig. 7.6).

In 2017, ZLCs used equity financing, debt financing, equity pledge and other financing channels to achieve the net financing of 226.3 billion yuan, down 8% from 2016 (Fig. 7.7).

Net investment was derived from the cash flow from investing activities in the consolidated cash flow statement of the listed companies' annual report. In 2017, the net investment of ZLCs reached 457.3 billion yuan, up 12% from 2016 (Fig. 7.8).

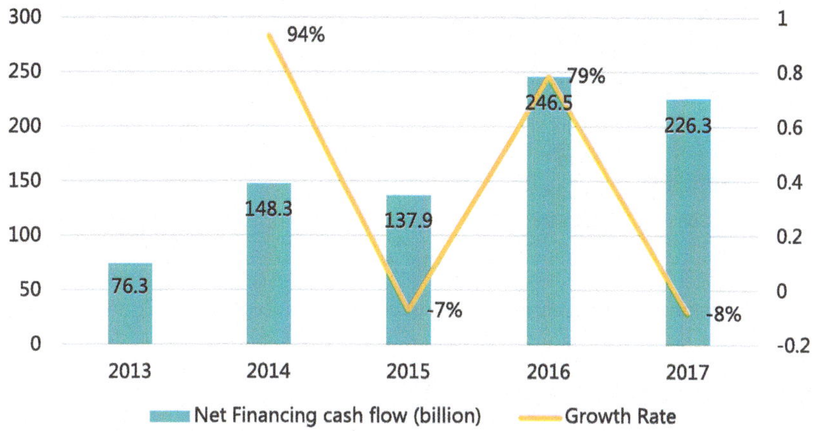


**Fig. 7.7** Changes of net financing cash flow of ZLCs in 2013–2017 (¥ billions)

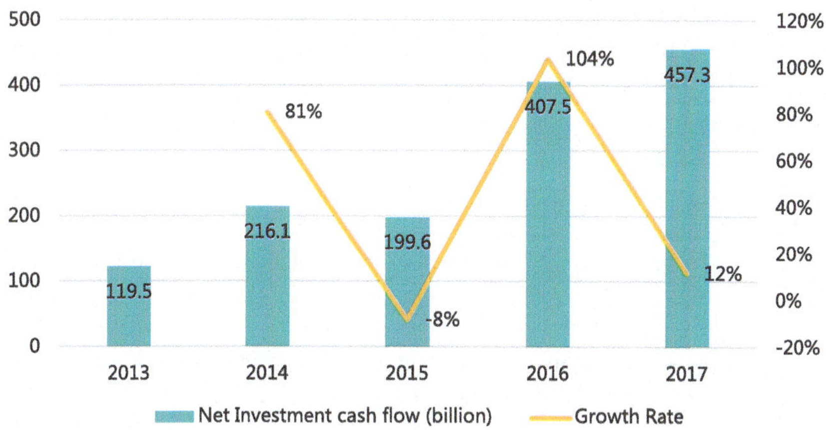


**Fig. 7.8** Changes of net investment cash flow of ZLCs in 2013–2017 (¥ billions)

## 7.3 Analysis of Financing Situation

### *7.3.1 IPO Proceeds of ZLCs in 2017*

In 2017, 25 ZLCs were listed and completed the initial public offerings, down 6% year-on-year. In terms of the number of companies, Z-Park companies preferred China A-share market, among which 20 were listed in China and 5 were listed overseas. Among the total IPO proceeds of 13.1 billion yuan, 6.8 billion yuan was from domestic stock market with 5.8 billion yuan from US stock market and 0.4 billion yuan from Hong Kong stock market. Among them, proceeds in NYSE accounted for

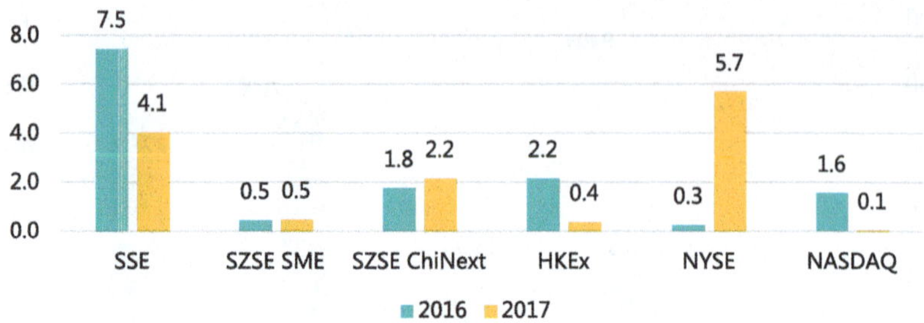


**Fig. 7.9** Comparison between each capital market on IPO proceeds of ZLCs in 2016–2017 (¥ billions)

**Table 7.1** IPO financing data of ZLCs in 2017

| | Number of ZLCs | Fund raised from IPO (¥ billions) | Accounting for the total amount of IPO financing (%) | Average IPO proceeds (¥ billions) |
|---|---|---|---|---|
| SSE | 10 | 4.1 | 31 | 0.408 |
| SZSE ChiNext | 8 | 2.2 | 17 | 0.275 |
| NYSE | 3 | 5.7 | 44 | 1.916 |
| SZSE SME | 2 | 0.5 | 4 | 0.265 |
| HKEx | 1 | 0.4 | 3 | 0.425 |
| NASDAQ | 1 | 0.1 | 1 | 0.092 |
| Total | 25 | 13.1 | 100 | 0.523 |

the largest proportion, namely 43.95%. And the average IPO proceeds in NYSE was the highest, at 1.916 billion yuan (Fig. 7.9 and Tables 7.1, 7.2).

### 7.3.2 *Proceeds Provided by Private Placements of ZLCs in 2017*

Taking the announcement date of private placements as statistical caliber, there were 29 ZLCs that successfully completed 39 times (declining by 43% year-on-year) of private placements, accounting for 8% of the total times of private placements of China A-share market in 2017. The total proceeds of ZLCs' private placements in 2017 was 39.8 billion yuan (down 77% y-o-y), representing 4% of total proceeds from private placements of China A-share market in 2017. From the two dimensions of quantity and amount, private placements of ZLCs were concentrated in SZSE (Tables 7.3, 7.4).

**Table 7.2** The IPO situation of new ZLCs in 2017

| No. | Securities code | Securities abbreviation | Listing location | IPO proceeds (¥ billions) |
|---|---|---|---|---|
| 1 | SOGO.N | SOGOU | NYSE | 3.9 |
| 2 | JT.N | JIANPU TECHNOLOGY | NYSE | 1.2 |
| 3 | 601858.SH | CSPM | SSE | 0.9 |
| 4 | 603803.SH | RAISECOM | SSE | 0.8 |
| 5 | RYB.N | RYB EDUCATION | NYSE | 0.7 |
| 6 | 603825.SH | HYLINK | SSE | 0.6 |
| 7 | 300719.SZ | ANDAWELL | SZSE | 0.5 |
| 8 | 300661.SZ | SGMICRO | SZSE | 0.4 |
| 9 | 1789.HK | AK MEDICAL | SEHK | 0.4 |
| 10 | 603970.SH | SINO-AGRI LEADING BIOSCIENCES | SSE | 0.4 |
| 11 | 002878.SZ | YUANLONG YATO | SZSE | 0.3 |
| 12 | 300608.SZ | SI-TECH | SZSE | 0.3 |
| 13 | 603603.SH | POTEN ENVIRO | SSE | 0.3 |
| 14 | 603860.SH | ROADMAINT | SSE | 0.3 |
| 15 | 002893.SZ | BEIJING HUAYUAN YITONG THERMAL TECHNOLOGY | SZSE | 0.3 |
| 16 | 603127.SH | JOINN | SSE | 0.3 |
| 17 | 603903.SH | CSD WATER SERVICE | SSE | 0.3 |
| 18 | 300663.SZ | CSII | SZSE | 0.2 |
| 19 | 603138.SH | VASTDATA | SSE | 0.2 |
| 20 | 300593.SZ | SUPLET | SZSE | 0.2 |
| 21 | 300688.SZ | DARKHORSE | SZSE | 0.2 |
| 22 | 300667.SZ | BEETECH | SZSE | 0.2 |
| 23 | 300684.SZ | JONES | SZSE | 0.2 |
| 24 | 603533.SH | IREADER TECHNOLOGY | SSE | 0.2 |
| 25 | RETO.O | RETO ECO-SOLUTIONS | NASDAQ | 0.1 |

*Source* WIND

**Table 7.3** Data of private placements of ZLCs in 2016–2017

| Sector | No. of PP of ZLCs | | | Capital raised from PP (¥ billions) | | |
|---|---|---|---|---|---|---|
| | 2016 | 2017 | Growth rate YOY (%) | 2016 | 2017 | Growth rate (%) |
| SSE | 8 | 4 | −50 | 80.7 | 5.7 | −93 |
| SZSE total | 61 | 35 | −43 | 89.4 | 34.1 | −62 |
| - Main board | 10 | 11 | 10 | 33.6 | 17 | −49 |
| - SME | 12 | 11 | −8 | 9.2 | 12.2 | 33 |
| - ChiNext | 39 | 13 | −67 | 46.6 | 7.3 | −84 |
| Total | 69 | 39 | −43 | 170.1 | 39.8 | −77 |

*Source* WIND. The capital raised from private placements didn't exclude the cost

**Table 7.4** 2017 private placements data of total China A-share market and ZLCs

| Capital market | No. of PP of ZLCs | | | Fund raised from PP | | |
|---|---|---|---|---|---|---|
| | Number of PP of A-share listed companies | No. of PP of ZLCs | ZLCs(%) | From total A-share listed companies (billion yuan) | From ZLCs (billion yuan) | ZLCs(%) |
| SSE | 159 | 4 | 3 | 570.0 | 5.7 | 1 |
| SZSE total | 352 | 35 | 10 | 449.7 | 34.1 | 8 |
| - Main board | 62 | 11 | 18 | 148.3 | 17.0 | 11 |
| - SME | 169 | 11 | 7 | 210.7 | 12.2 | 6 |
| - ChiNext | 121 | 13 | 11 | 90.7 | 7.3 | 8 |
| Total | 511 | 39 | 8 | 1019.7 | 39.8 | 4 |

*Source* WIND. The capital raised from private placements didn't exclude the cost

### 7.3.3 *Proceeds Provided by Bond Issuance of ZLCs in 2017*

After the great bull market in 2015–2016, the bond market gradually cooled down in 2017. Under the stringent financial supervision and deleveraging, domestic bond financing also shrank. Affected by the overall environment, the bond financing situation of ZLCs in 2017 was not optimistic as well. In 2017, 21 ZLCs issued 30 corporate bonds in the stock exchanges, with the number of bond issues dropping by 58% y-o-y. The total amount of capitals raised reached 29.2 billion yuan, down 74% y-o-y (Table 7.5).

From the perspective of the classification of corporate bonds, ZLCs issued 22 public company bonds in 2017, accounting for 4.10% of the total number of public company bonds issued in China A-share market, and raised 24.4 billion yuan,

**Table 7.5** Data of bond financing of ZLCs in 2016–2017

| Bond categories | Number of bonds | | | Capital raised from bonds (¥ billions) | | |
|---|---|---|---|---|---|---|
| | 2016 | 2017 | Growth rate (%) | 2016 | 2017 | Growth rate (%) |
| Public company bond | 46 | 22 | −52 | 72.1 | 24.4 | −66 |
| Private equity bond | 26 | 8 | −69 | 39.9 | 4.8 | −88 |
| Total | 72 | 30 | −58 | 112 | 29.2 | −74 |

**Table 7.6** Data of bond financing of China A-share market and ZLCs in 2017

| Bond categories | Number of bonds | | | Capital raised from bonds (¥ billions) | | |
|---|---|---|---|---|---|---|
| | A-share market | ZLCs | ZLCs (%) | A-share market | ZLCs | ZLCs (%) |
| Public company bonds | 537 | 22 | 4.10 | 563.7 | 24.4 | 4.33 |
| Private equity bonds | 654 | 8 | 1.22 | 529.9 | 4.8 | 0.91 |
| Total | 1191 | 30 | 2.52 | 1093.6 | 29.2 | 2.67 |

accounting for 4.33% of the total amount of public company bonds issued in China A-share market. ZLCs issued 8 private equity bonds, accounting for 1.22% of the total amount of private equity bonds issued in China A-share market, and raised 4.8 billion yuan, accounting for 0.91% of the total amount of private equity bonds issued in China A-share market (Table 7.6).

### 7.3.4 *Equity Pledge Status of ZLCs in 2017*

According to statistics from Choice, 1291 equity pledge transactions were conducted by 138 ZLCs in 2017, with 19.9 billion shares pledged and a reference market capitalisation of 283.7 billion yuan. Compared with the same period of 2016, the number of equity pledge transactions increased by 27% (1016 equity pledge transactions in 2016), the number of pledged stocks increased by 11% (17.9 billion shares were traded in 2016), and the reference market capitalisation of the stocks involved also increased by 11% (255.9 billion yuan of reference market capitalisation was involved in the first half of 2017).

Statistics showed that the ZLCs that conducted equity pledge transactions concentrated on GEB. Among them, there were 28 ZLCs on the main board, 36 on the SME and 74 on the GEB. In addition, from the number and the market capitalisation of pledged stocks, listed companies on GEB still played a dominant role. This fea-

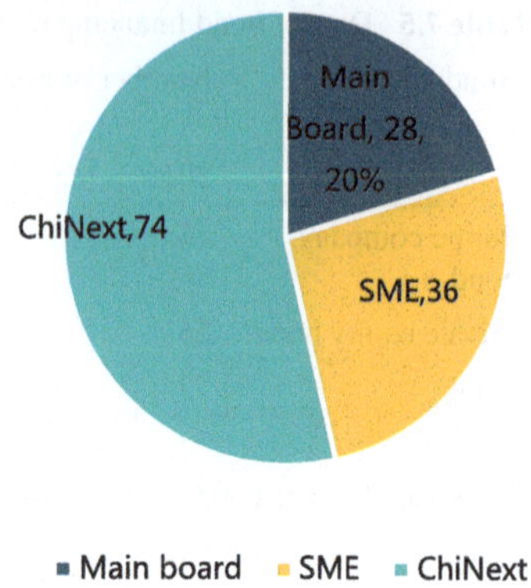


**Fig. 7.10** Data of ZLCs conducting equity pledge transactions in different sectors in 2017

**Table 7.7** Equity pledge status of ZLCs in each capital market in 2017

| Sector | Number of ZLCs | | The number of shares pledged | | The market capitalisation of shares pledged | |
|---|---|---|---|---|---|---|
| | Number | Percentage | Number (billions of units ) | Percentage | Market capitalisation (¥ billions) | Percentage |
| ChiNext | 74 | 54 | 7.8 | 39 | 105 | 37 |
| SME | 36 | 26 | 6.1 | 31 | 82.2 | 29 |
| Main board | 28 | 20 | 6 | 30 | 96.9 | 34 |
| Total | 138 | 100 | 19.9 | 100 | 284 | 100 |

*Source* Choice

ture was different from the group characteristics of listed companies that had equity pledge transactions in the China A-share market (Among the listed companies that had equity pledge transactions in A-share market in 2017, there were 796 companies listed on the main board, 637 companies listed on the SME and 555 companies listed on the GEB), which shows that GEB listed companies are more active in the group of ZLC (Fig. 7.10).

In addition, from the perspective of risk, 20% of the equity pledge transactions conducted by ZLCs (252 transactions in total) had reached "open line" and were facing liquidation crisis. This proportion was slightly lower than that in China (25%) and in Beijing (21%) (Table 7.7).

# Chapter 8
# Human Resources Status and Tax Expenses of ZLCs in 2017

## 8.1 Employees in ZLCs in 2017

By the end of 2017, ZLCs employed totally 2.052 million people, an increase of 110 thousand employees compared to the previous year (a 6% growth year-on-year) (Fig. 8.1).

The number of employees in domestic listed companies accounted for the largest proportion of the total number of employees in ZLCs, over 50%, followed by HK listed companies and U.S. listed companies. There were 1.213 million employees from domestic listed companies, 59% of the total number of employees in ZLCs; there were 455 thousand employees from HK listed companies, 22% of the total number of employees in ZLCs; there were 384 thousand people employed by U.S. listed companies, 19% of the total number of employees in ZLCs (Fig. 8.2).

In terms of industries, 31% of employees (640 thousand) were in the industrials, followed by 26% (540 thousand) in the information technology and 20% (410 thousand) in the consumer discretionary. With a large number of employees, the three industries contributed 1.59 million jobs, accounting for 77% of the total number of

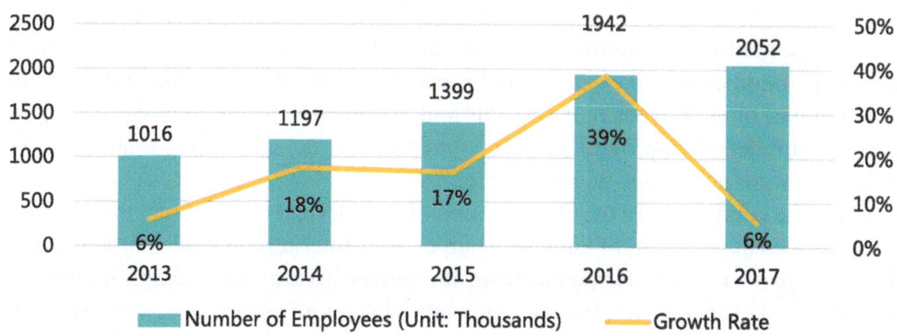


**Fig. 8.1** Changes of employee status in ZLCs in 2013–2017


Zhongguancun Listed Companies Association, *The Competitiveness Report of Zhongguancun Listed Companies (2018)*,
https://doi.org/10.1007/978-981-13-7697-9_8

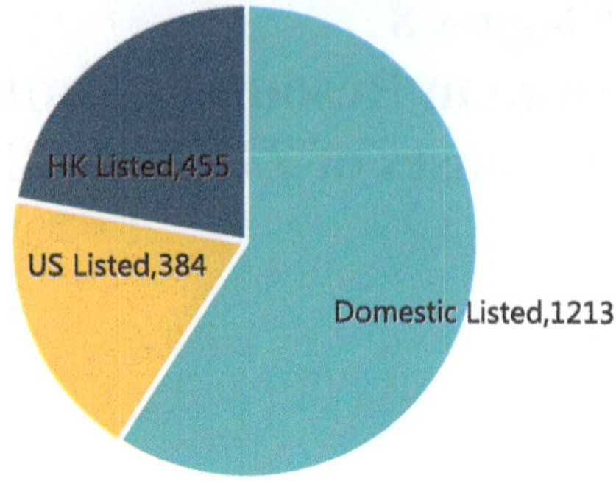


**Fig. 8.2** The component of employees in ZLCs in 2017 (Unit: Thousands)

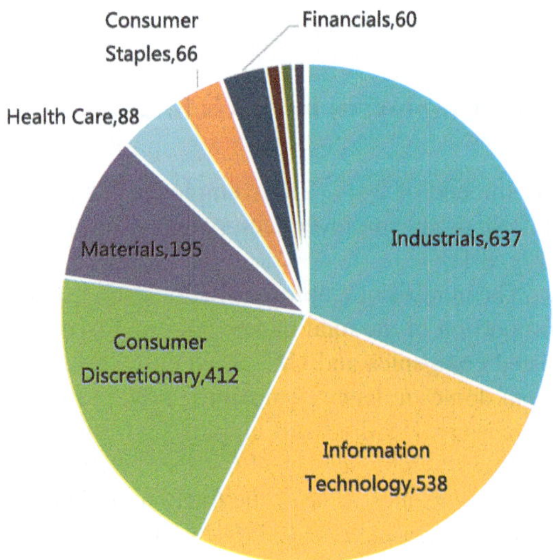


**Fig. 8.3** The employee distribution of each industries in 2017 (Unit: Thousands)

employees in ZLCs. This fact highlighted the economic and social influence from these three industries on ZLCs (Fig. 8.3).

According to the distribution of the average number of employees in each industry, the average number of employees in companies of financial industry was the highest, while that number in real estate is the lowest. It was worth noting that although the total number of employees in industrials and information technology was large, the average number of employees in each company was not, indicating that these two industries were not labour-intensive (Fig. 8.4).

From the perspective of the classification of Internet and non-Internet industries, it could be seen that in terms of human resources, non-Internet companies still occupied the main part of ZLCs. However, from the perspective of the average number of employees of each industry, Internet companies had more advantages, which to some extent indicated that Internet companies were generally larger in scale (Table 8.1).

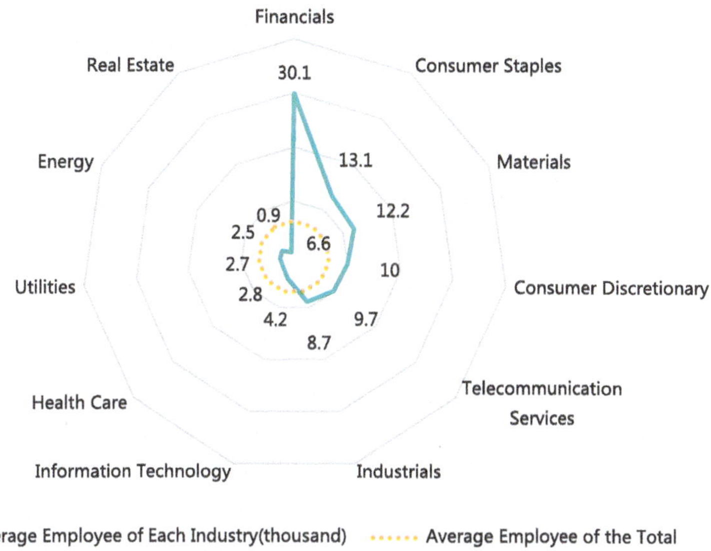


**Fig. 8.4** ZLCs' average of employees in each industry in 2017 (Unit: Hundreds)

**Table 8.1** The employee distribution of Internet/Non-Internet of ZLCs in 2017

| | Employee (thousand) | Employee (%) | Number of ZLC | Average number of employee |
|---|---|---|---|---|
| Internet | 320 | 15 | 41 | 7718 |
| Non-internet | 1740 | 85 | 271 | 6404 |
| Total | 2050 | 100 | 312 | 6571 |

## 8.2 Human Resources Output of ZLCs in 2017

In 2017, the per capita revenue of ZLCs reached 194.4 thousand yuan, an increase of 8% over the previous year. Per capita net profit had the same trend with per capita revenue, reaching 8.18 thousand yuan, an increase of 8% over the previous year. The per capita income tax paid increased) to 2.74 thousand yuan, up by 34% from the previous year (Fig. 8.5).

From the perspective of industry, the per capita income of Real Estate was the highest. Correspondingly, its per capita net profit and income tax were much higher than those of other industries. Compared with the per capita GDP of Beijing in 2017 (12.9 thousand yuan), Consumer Staples with the lowest per capita income among these industries was still 4.5 times of the per capita GDP of Beijing, which to some extent showed the great contribution made by human resources of ZLCs to economic activity and the growth of economy. In addition to Real Estate, the per capita net profit of Utilities and Health Care was also relatively high, which was closely related to the improvement of production efficiency brought about by the generally higher

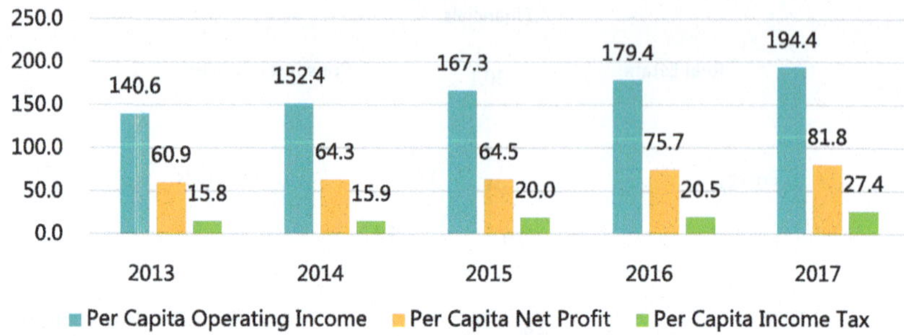


**Fig. 8.5** Per capita revenue of ZLCs from 2013 to 2017 (Unit: Thousand)

**Table 8.2** Per capita resource output of industries in ZLCs (Unit: Thousand)

| Industry | Per capita operating income | Per capita net profit | Per capita income tax |
|---|---|---|---|
| Real estate | 9924.7 | 548.6 | 539.9 |
| Financials | 5274.0 | 77.3 | 43.2 |
| Industrials | 2407.7 | 103.7 | 27.0 |
| Utilities | 2331.2 | 380.0 | 77.9 |
| Telecommunication services | 1814.8 | 181.9 | 40.0 |
| Consumer discretionary | 1805.1 | 51.8 | 21.4 |
| Information technology | 1671.4 | 62.1 | 28.3 |
| Materials | 1241.1 | 74.2 | 27.9 |
| Health care | 1224.1 | 167.3 | 35.4 |
| Energy | 801.4 | 43.2 | 20.1 |
| Consumer staples | 563.5 | 22.4 | 6.9 |

technical and professional level of the industry. At the same time, due to the strong profitability per capita, the per capita income tax paid by Utilities was also relatively high, and its contribution to fiscal revenue was relatively high as well (Table 8.2).

## 8.3 Income Tax Expenses of ZLCs in 2017

As of the end of 2017, the income tax expenses of ZLCs was 56.3 billion yuan, an increase of 16.4 billion yuan compared to the previous year. It was speculated that it was resulted from the increase of newly added ZLCs which increased by 25% compared with 2016. In 2017, corporate income tax in Beijing totalled 122.98 billion yuan, of which 46% was paid by ZLCs (Fig. 8.6).

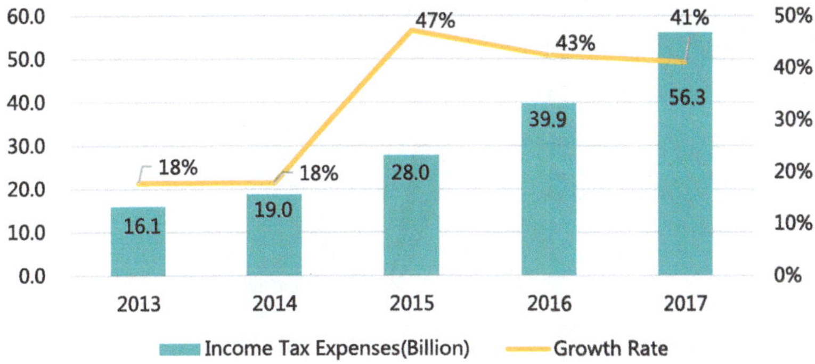


**Fig. 8.6** The income tax expenses of ZLCs from 2013 to 2017

**Fig. 8.7** The composition of income tax of ZLCs in 2017

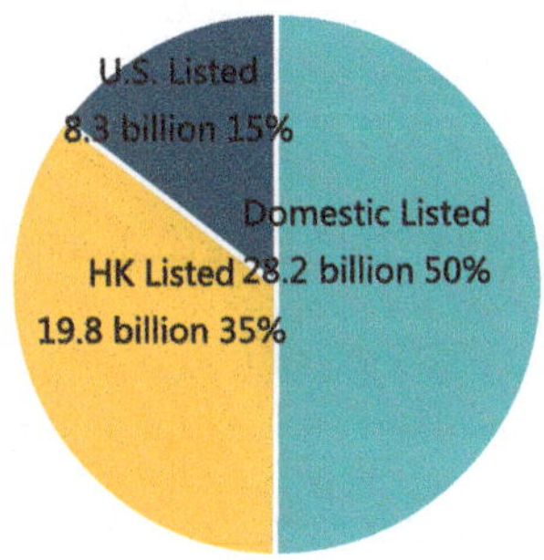


The income tax of domestic listed companies accounted for the largest proportion of ZLCs, accounting for half, with Hong Kong and the U.S. listed companies following the list. Specifically, the total income tax of listed companies in China was 28.2 billion yuan, accounting for 50% of the total income tax of ZLCs. The income tax of listed companies in Hong Kong stock market was 19.8 billion yuan, accounting for 35% of the total income tax of ZLCs. The tax on U.S. listed companies was 8.3 billion yuan, or 15% of ZLCs' total (Figs. 8.7, 8.8 and 8.9).

From the perspective of industry classification, the total amount of income tax paid by Industrials, Information Technology and Consumer Discretionary were the highest, while the average income tax paid by Financials was the highest, and the distribution of other industries was relatively uniform.

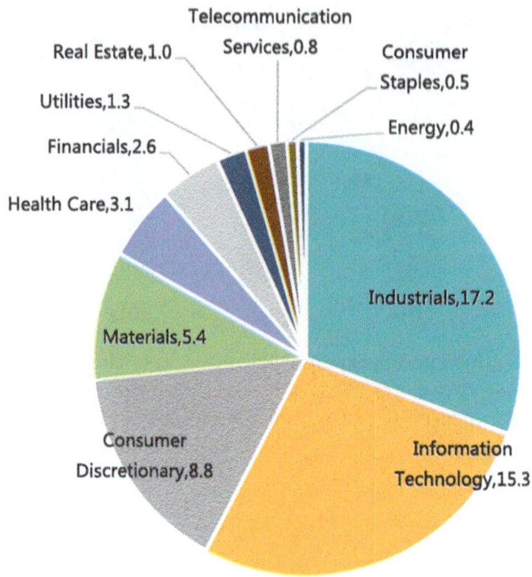


**Fig. 8.8** The income tax distribution of each industry in 2017 (Unit: Billion)

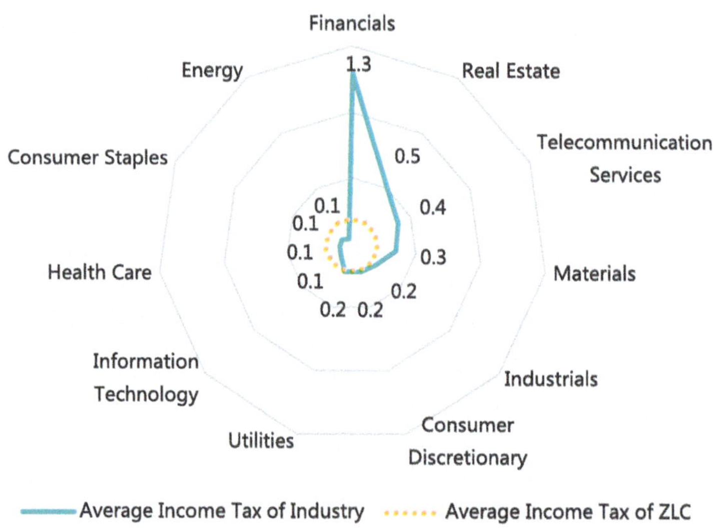


**Fig. 8.9** Average income tax of industry of ZLCs in 2017 (Unit: Billion)

# Chapter 9
# Analysis of Dominant Industries at Zhongguancun

According to the Wind Industry Classification Standard (WICS), Zhongguancun listed companies involved 11 industries. Based on the analysis of the key indicators from an industrial perspective mentioned above, it could be seen that ZLCs would be mainly classified in four industries of Information Technology, Industrials, Consumer Discretionary and Health Care, within which there were a great number of large businesses that output products in massive quantities. As public companies always lead an industry, and can reflect its overall development and scale, the distribution of ZLCs could reflect Zhongguancun's regional economy structure to a certain extent. Therefore, the analysis of economic trends of dominant industries would explain how Zhongguancun achieved its economic transformation from the perspective of public companies.

## 9.1 Scale Change Analysis

In terms of the absolute number, IT industry has a larger amount of companies than the other three industries over the years with a steadily growing by about 9% a year. Meanwhile, the number of industrials companies has seen a rapid growth, having surpassed the number of companies in the Consumer Discretionary and Health Care industries and almost caught up with the IT industry. Health Care industry had fewest companies and a relatively low growth rate. In general, in terms of the scale change of dominant industries from 2013 to 2017, the Information Technology industry has taken the largest share, but its proportion has been continuously shrinking. The number of Industrials enterprises has been increasing rapidly with a large room for growth and a growing proportion. The number of companies in the Health Care industry almost stayed the same with a slow growth rate and a stable proportion (Fig. 9.1).



Zhongguancun Listed Companies Association, *The Competitiveness Report of Zhongguancun Listed Companies (2018)*,
https://doi.org/10.1007/978-981-13-7697-9_9

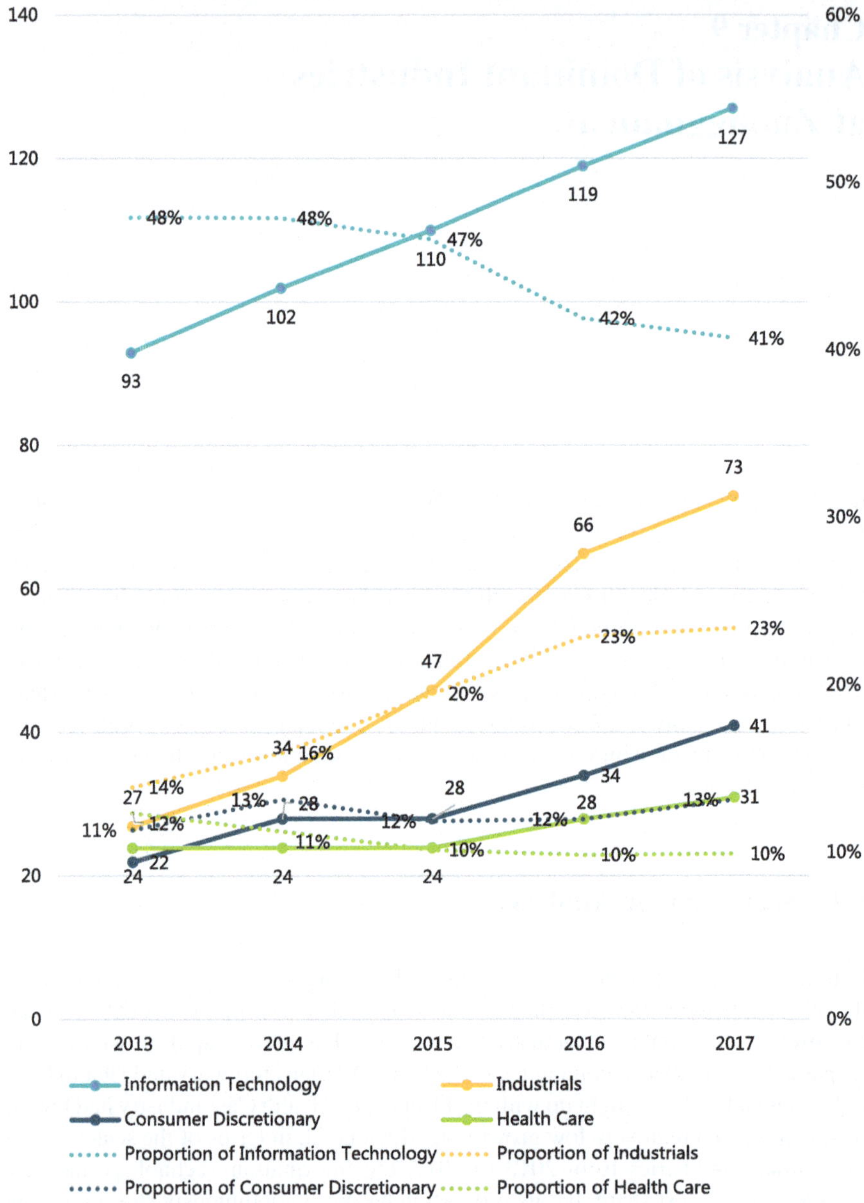


**Fig. 9.1** The number of ZLCs in dominant industries (2013–2017)

In terms of the changes in market cap over the past five years, the total market capitalisation of Information Technology, Industrials, Consumer Discretionary, and Health Care have been rising for five consecutive years. Among them, the market cap of the Consumer Discretionary industry had the highest compound growth rate, reaching 58%; the market cap growth rates of the Information Technology, Industrials and Health Care industries were 18, 45 and 20% respectively. In terms of proportion, the market cap proportion of the Information Technology industry has been declining year by year; the market cap proportion of Industrials and Consumer Discretionary have steadily increased; the market cap proportion of the Health Care industry was the most stable. Although the total market cap was relatively low, the Health Care industry enjoyed a highly stable growth. The changes of the market cap proportions of dominant industries reflected a slowdown of the overall growth of the Information Technology industry to a certain extent, that other dominant industries have gradually gained more room for growth, and that the industrial structure of ZLCs started changing (Fig. 9.2).

## 9.2 Output Scale Analysis

### *9.2.1 Revenue Analysis*

According to the changes in revenue and its proportion, the Industrials industry had the fastest growth in revenue, followed by the Consumer Discretionary industry. Proportions of Information Technology and Industrials industry in the total revenue of ZLCs have declined. By contrast, the proportion of revenue in Consumer Discretionary industry has steadily increased. According to the revenue in 2013 and 2017, we could see that IT industry and Industrials industry were the largest industries by revenue in early days but the gap narrowed later on. In general, the revenue of the Consumer Discretionary industry has been growing rapidly and had great growth potential (Fig. 9.3).

### *9.2.2 Net Profit Analysis*

The net profit and net profit proportions' changes of dominant industries feature a sharp net profit decrease of the IT industry and by contrast the rapid net profit increase of the Industrials industry. The net profit of the IT industry has gradually declined after reaching its peak in 2015, which led to a rapid decline in its share in the overall net profit. At the same time, the profitability of Industrials companies has been gradually rising, which has surpassed the Information Technology industry in 2016 and become the main net profit contributor among ZLCs. The Consumer

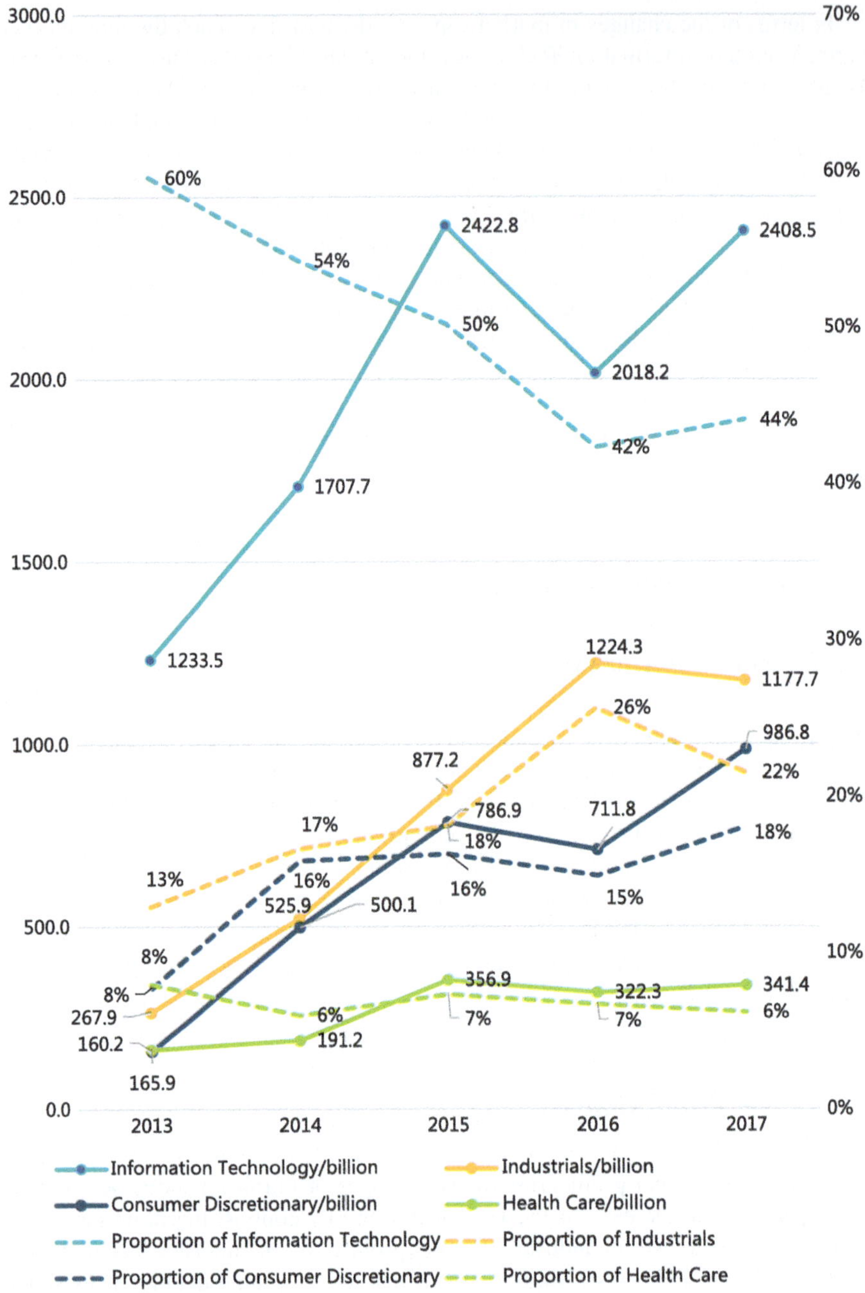


**Fig. 9.2** The market cap of ZLCs in dominant industries (2013–2017)

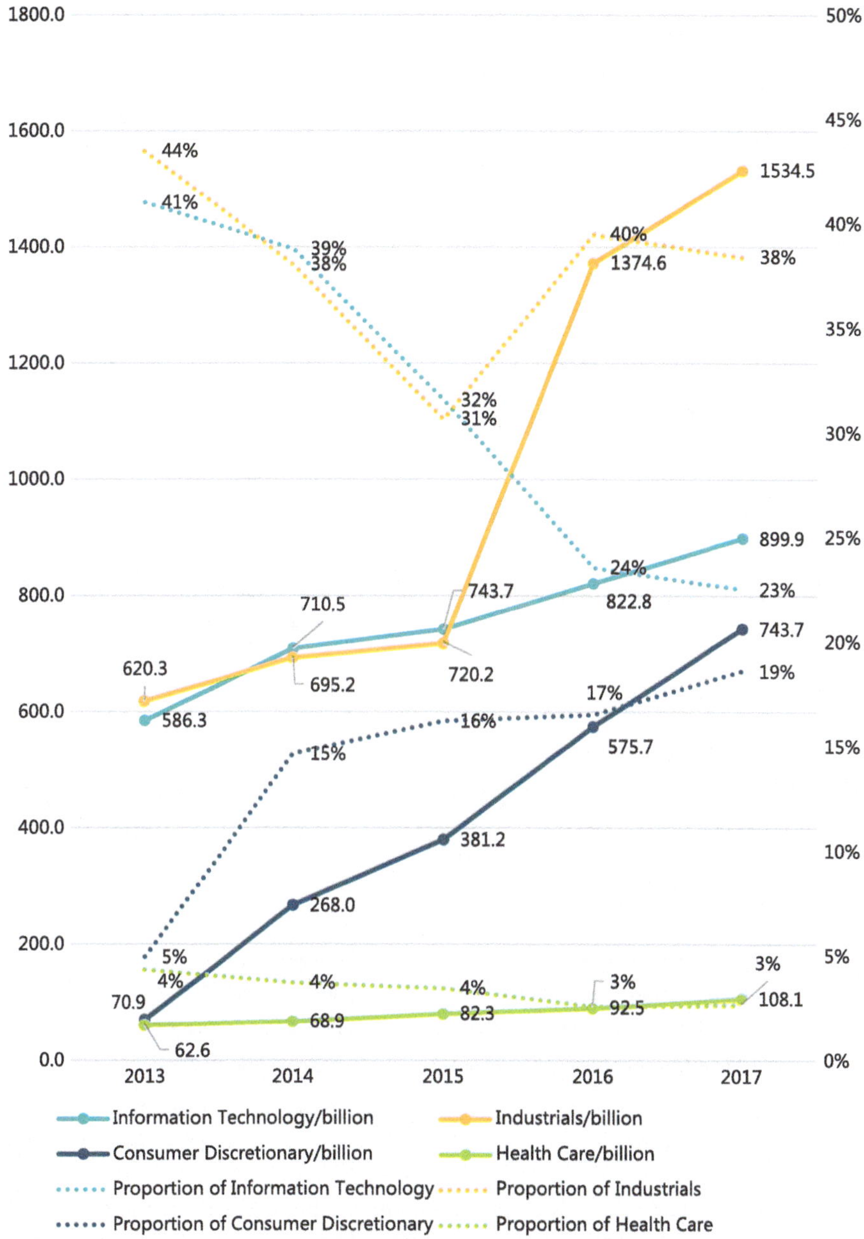


**Fig. 9.3** The revenue of ZLCs in dominant industries (2013–2017)

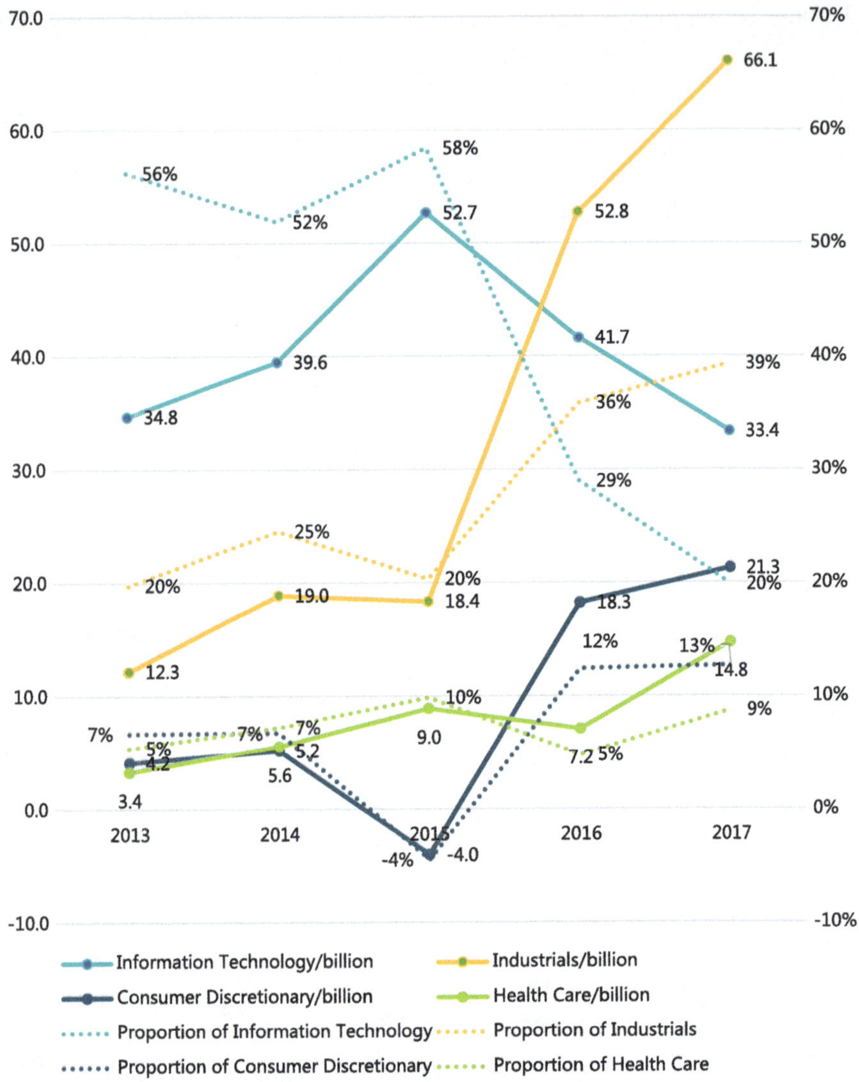


**Fig. 9.4** The net profit of ZLCs in dominant industries (2013–2017)

Discretionary industry has also achieved relatively high growth, while the Health Care industry maintained a steady development (Fig. 9.4).

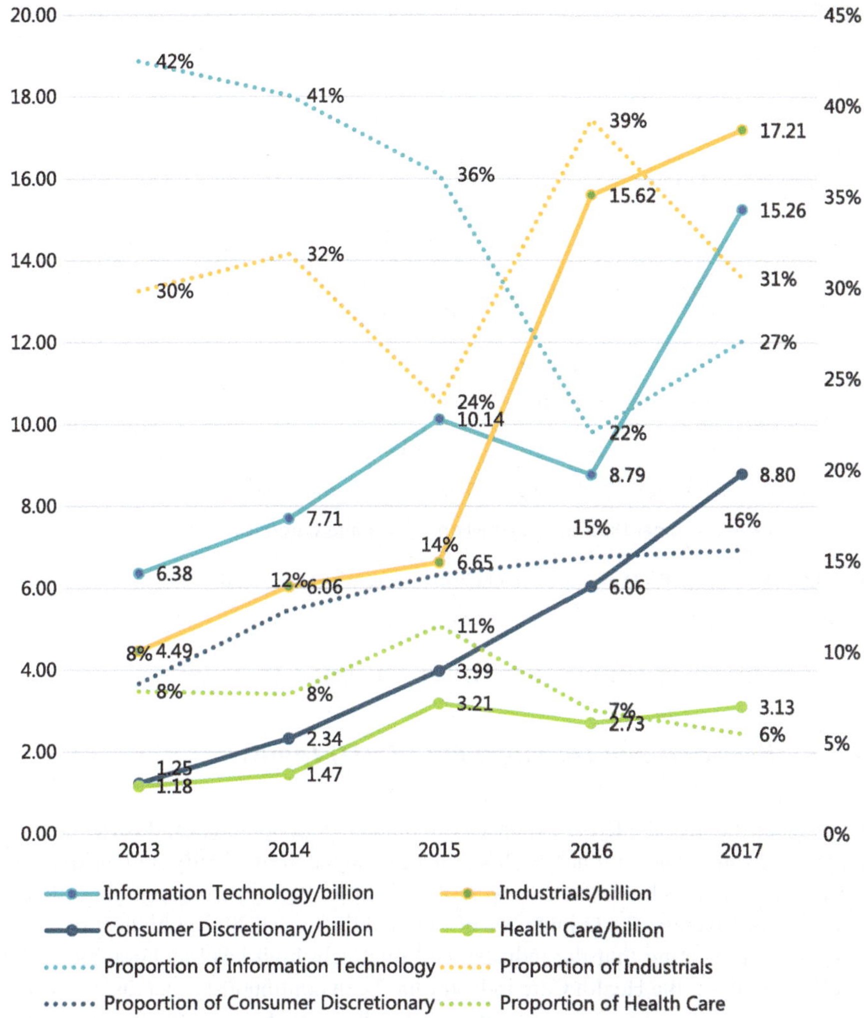


**Fig. 9.5** The income tax of ZLCs in dominant industries (2013–2017)

### *9.2.3 Income Tax Analysis*

The income tax of the four industries has continued to grow over the years. Since 2016, Industrials industry has surpassed IT industry to be the largest taxpayer at Zhongguancun. Such a shift had a close relationship with its enhanced profitability, and reflected that public companies in the Industrials industry at Zhongguancun would contribute more in the future (Fig. 9.5).

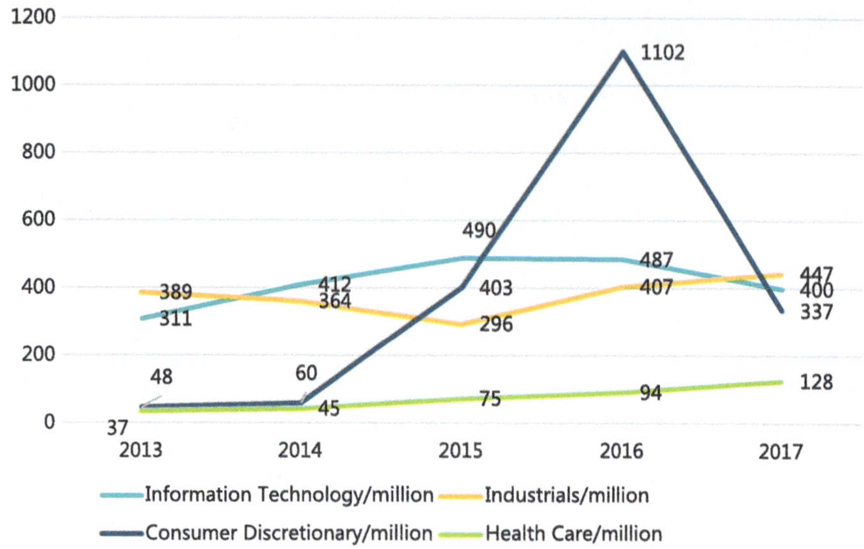


**Fig. 9.6** The average R&D expenses of ZLCs in dominant industries (2013–2017)

## 9.3 Analysis of Innovation Input-Output Efficiency

### *9.3.1 Research and Development (R&D) Inputs*

In terms of the average R&D expenses of companies in dominant industries, trends for the Consumer Discretionary industry have changed dramatically, and the average R&D expenses in other industries were less volatile. From the perspective of R&D intensity, the average R&D intensity of the IT industry has hit the highest over the past years, indicating that the industry had relatively high-level technologies. The R&D intensity of the Health Care industry has been continuously increasing, which directly reflected that technical innovation has been paid more attention to in this industry (Figs. 9.6 and 9.7).

### *9.3.2 Per Capita Outputs*

The per capita revenue can reflect the production efficiency of a company or industry to a certain extent. The trend of the per capita revenue of the dominant industries at Zhongguancun has changed from 2013 to 2017, reflecting that the Industrials industry had both the highest per capita revenue and the highest employees' production efficiency, and the two numbers have been continuedly rising after 2015. The per

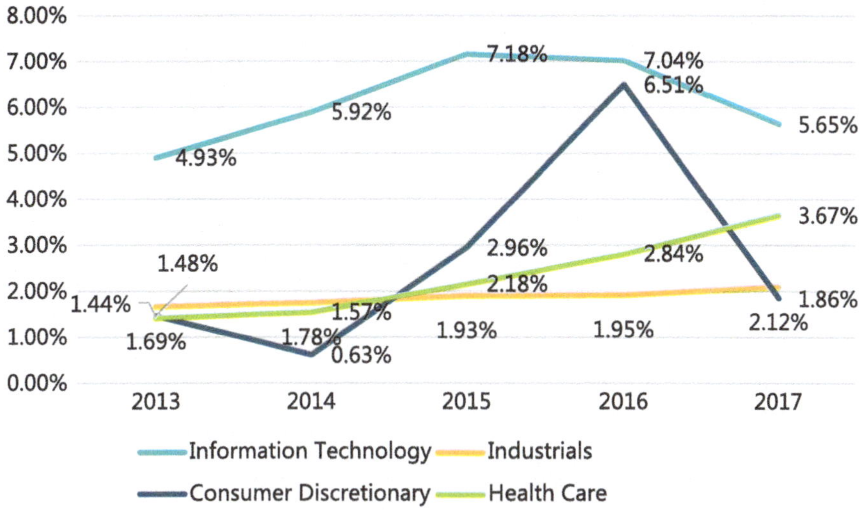


**Fig. 9.7** The R&D intensity of ZLCs in dominant industries (2013–2017)

capita revenue of the Consumer Discretionary industry has been climbing rapidly, and its production efficiency has been greatly improved.

The per capita net profit changes in dominant industries were volatile. Overall, the per capita net profit growth of the Health Care industry was the fastest. In 2017, it has far surpassed other industries, reaching 170,000 yuan, but its volatility was relatively high. The per capita net profit of the Information Technology industry has shown a downward trend. The per capita net profit of Industrials industry has increased steadily, and reached 100,000 yuan in 2017.

Generally speaking, the per capita corporate income tax of dominant industries has increased. Among them, the Health Care industry had the highest annual growth rate and a relatively high volatility. The per capita corporate income tax of the Information Technology industry went down in 2016. However, as multiple IT subsidiaries were founded in the U.S. and their corporate incomes were affected by the US tax reform, the per capita corporate income tax increased significantly compared to the same period of the last year though its per capita net profit declined in 2017 (Figs. 9.8, 9.9 and 9.10).

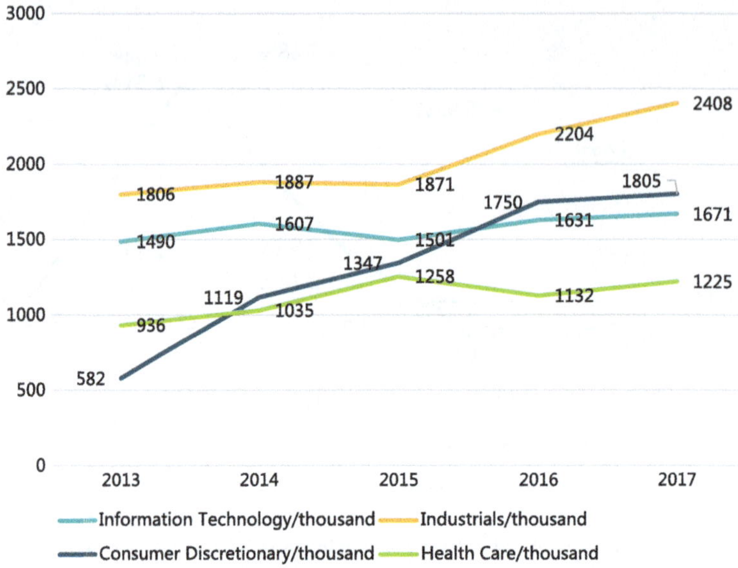


**Fig. 9.8** The per capita revenue of ZLCs in dominant industries (2013–2017)

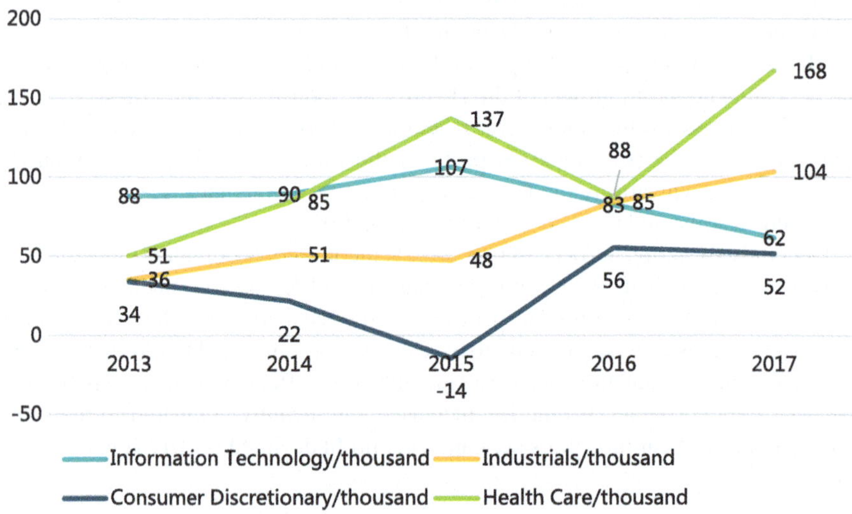


**Fig. 9.9** The per capita net profit of ZLCs in dominant industries (2013–2017)

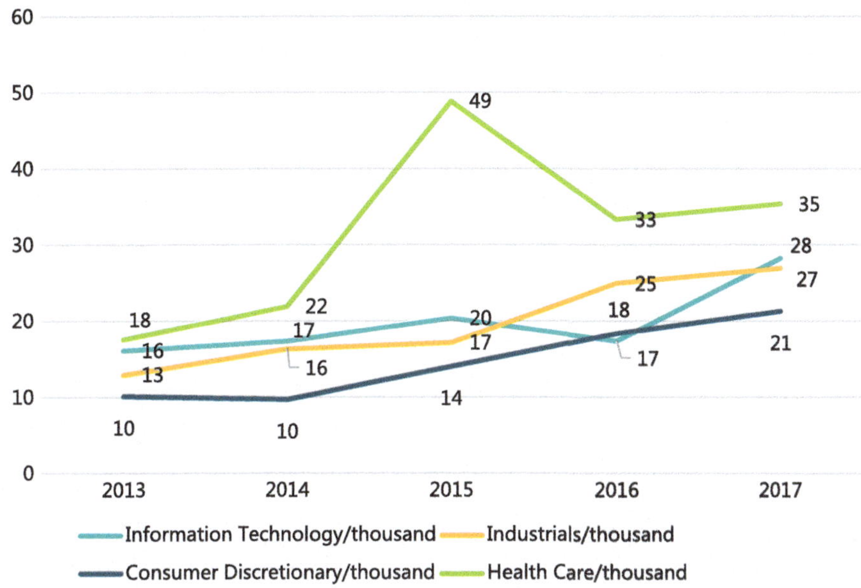


**Fig. 9.10** The per capita income tax of ZLCs in dominant industries (2013–2017)

# Chapter 10
# Status of Continuous Trading ZLCs

ZLCs have witnessed great developments, getting public and trading on the international stock market. In order to have a better understanding of ZLCs' developments, the report does not cover companies listed in 2017 and those going private. In this report, business data from 281 ZLCs listed in 2016 will be discussed.

Although the market cap of ZLCs has been fluctuating quite a bit, the industrial scale was growing rapidly. The total market cap of 281 ZLCs rose from 4741.5 billion yuan in 2016 to 5207.6 billion yuan in 2017, an increase of 9.8% y-o-y, among which 110 companies had a market cap of more than 10 billion yuan, compared to 127 companies in 2016. The total assets have increased from 5680.6 billion yuan in 2016 to 6301.5 billion yuan in 2017, up 10.9% y-o-y. Among them, 83 companies, compared to 74 in 2016, had total assets of over 10 billion yuan (see Table 10.1).

The profitability of ZLCs has been continuously growing. The total revenue of 281 ZLCs has increased by 13.5% since last year, from 3468.8 billion yuan in 2016 to 3937.2 billion yuan in 2017. Among them, 75 ZLCs' revenue exceeded 5 billion yuan. This has increased, from 72 in the previous year. The total gross profits reached

**Table 10.1** Scale of 281 continuous trading ZLCs (2016–2017)

| Capital markets | No. of ZLCs | Market cap. (in billion yuan) | | Total assets (in billion yuan) | | Growth rate (%) | |
|---|---|---|---|---|---|---|---|
| | | 2016 | 2017 | 2016 | 2017 | Market cap. | Total assets |
| Domestic | 200 | 3310.4 | 3153.8 | 3365.3 | 3767.1 | −5 | 11.9 |
| Overseas | 81 | 1431.1 | 2053.8 | 2315.3 | 2534.4 | 43.5 | 9.4 |
| – US | 30 | 960.6 | 1504.2 | 568.6 | 723.5 | 56.6 | 27.2 |
| – HK | 51 | 470.5 | 549.6 | 1746.7 | 1810.9 | 16.8 | 3.7 |
| Total | 281 | 4741.5 | 5207.6 | 5680.6 | 6301.5 | 9.8 | 10.9 |

Continuous trading companies refer to Zhongguancun listed companies that are on the stock market in 2016 and 2017.



Zhongguancun Listed Companies Association, *The Competitiveness Report of Zhongguancun Listed Companies (2018)*,
https://doi.org/10.1007/978-981-13-7697-9_10

784.9 billion yuan in 2017 from 672.7 billion yuan in 2016, up 16.7% y-o-y. Among 281 ZLCs, 64 of them held gross profits of over 2 billion yuan, an increase of 4 companies compared to 60 in 2016. The total net profits increased to 164.3 billion yuan from 147.0 billion yuan in 2016, an increase of 11.8% y-o-y. Among them, 69 companies had net profits of over 0.5 billion yuan, an increase of 8 companies compared to 61 in 2016 (see Table 10.2).

**Table 10.2** Profitability of 281 continuous trading ZLCs (2016–2017)

| Capital markets | Revenue (in billion yuan) | | Gross Profits (in billion yuan) | | Net profits (in billion yuan) | | Growth rate (%) | | |
|---|---|---|---|---|---|---|---|---|---|
| | 2016 | 2017 | 2016 | 2017 | 2016 | 2017 | Revenue | Gross profits | Net profits |
| Domestic | 1918.4 | 2163.9 | 341.2 | 391.6 | 93.0 | 92.2 | 12.8 | 14.8 | 0.8 |
| Overseas | 1550.4 | 1773.3 | 331.5 | 393.3 | 54.0 | 72.1 | 14.4 | 18.6 | 33.5 |
| – US | 427.7 | 562.0 | 123.3 | 161.4 | 10.0 | 23.2 | 31.4 | 30.9 | 132 |
| – HK and others | 1122.7 | 1211.3 | 208.2 | 231.9 | 44.0 | 48.9 | 7.9 | 11.4 | 11.1 |
| Total | 3468.8 | 3937.2 | 672.7 | 784.9 | 147.0 | 164.3 | 13.5 | 16.7 | 11.8 |

# Chapter 11
# Conclusion

## 11.1 The Fundamental Status of ZLCs in 2017

### *11.1.1 R&D Investment and Patent Output Continued Growing, and Corporate Innovation Capabilities Continued Rising*

In 2017, the R&D expenses of ZLCs totalled 122 billion yuan, increasing 18% y-o-y. The average R&D intensity was 3.31%, which increased by 12% y-o-y, and it was much higher than that of A-share companies (1.48%). Besides, nearly 30% of ZLCs (78 companies) had a R&D intensity of more than 10%, reaching an international high level. At the same time, the data for five consecutive years illustrated that the R&D intensity and the gross profit margin of ZLCs showed a significant positive correlation, which further indicated that innovation investment played an important role in improving the business performance of ZLCs.

At the same time, ZLCs filed more patents compared to the same period of last year. The number of patents that ZLCs filed was increasing for five consecutive years. In 2017, patent applications by these companies numbered 8857 (up 4% y-o-y), and granted patent applications reached 5435 (up 15% y-o-y). The total number of effective invention patents reached 12,888 (up 42% y-o-y), and PCT patent applications amounted to 1695 (up 5% year-on-year). The sustained and steady growth of patent output was due to the continuous investment in R&D, and an increasing corporate value showed its great significance. The continuous growth of R&D investment and patent output reflects the further improvement of the innovation efficiency and innovation capability of ZLCs.



Zhongguancun Listed Companies Association, *The Competitiveness Report of Zhongguancun Listed Companies (2018)*,
https://doi.org/10.1007/978-981-13-7697-9_11

### 11.1.2 Total Market Capitalisation Reached a New High, and Large-Volume Companies Stood Out

As of the end of 2017, the total market capitalisation of ZLCs reached 5458.9 billion yuan, up 15% y-o-y. That growth was higher than Chinese A-share companies (12.43%). In 2016, the total market capitalisation of ZLCs witnessed a decline for the first time affected by stagnant capital market environments. In 2017, ZLCs reported an increase in total market capitalisation of more than 5 trillion yuan, hitting a record high. That amount was nearly twice of Beijing's GDP (2800.04 billion yuan). ZLCs had a total capitalisation up by 70% y-o-y on U.C. stock market. Also the growth rate of the total market capitalisation of ZLCs listed on the NYSE and Nasdaq was higher than that of capital markets.

The distribution of market capitalisation of ZLCs maintained a superstar effect in the presence of the long tail. 20% companies held 70% of the total market capitalisation. A few large companies gathered a large number of market capitalisation and led regional economic development. 6 companies, accounting for 2% of ZLCs, held market capitalisation of more than 100 billion yuan (Baidu, Jingdong, BOE-B, CCCC, China Railway and Weibo). Their market capitalisation totalled 1632.2 billion yuan (account for 30% of the total market capitalisation). 108 companies had a market capitalisation within the range of 10 billion yuan and 100 billion yuan (35%). Their total market capitalisation reached 2959.7 billion yuan (54%). At the same time, there were a large number of fast-growing small and medium-sized ZLCs, which will contribute to the future development of Zhongguancun. 27 companies, which were mostly small and medium-sized companies in 2016 and accounted for 20% of the total (281 ZLCs), had a market capitalisation up by more than 50% compared to the same period of the last year.

### 11.1.3 Total Revenue and Total Net Profit Increased Steadily, and Technological Innovation Improved ZLCs' Capabilities to Create Profits

In 2017, the total revenue and total net profit of ZLCs were 3988.6 billion yuan and 167.8 billion yuan respectively, up 14% y-o-y. As China's economic growth has slowed down, the total revenue of ZLCs has been growing slowly compared to the same period of the last year. However, their revenue growth rate still exceeded that of Industrial companies above designated size (11.1%), indicating that Zhongguancun technological innovation companies has been growing. It is worth mentioning that among all ZLCs, leading Internet companies have announced an increase in net profit in 2017. 7 companies had (Baidu, Jingdong, 58 City, Cheetah, SouFun, Weibo and Momo) more than 1 billion yuan net profits, up more than 50%.

Both gross profit and gross profit margin of ZLCs have been continuously growing. In 2017, gross profit totalled 803.5 billion yuan, up 19% y-o-y, and gross profit margin reached 20.14%, up 0.71 percentage point. This group of figures reflected that ZLCs had better business performances. Among ZLCs, companies with higher gross profit margins mainly concentrated in the Information Technology industry and Health Care industry. These two industries had greater R&D intensity (Information Technology had a R&D intensity of 5.65%, and Health Care 3.67%), which illustrated that the technological innovation has greatly improved business performances.

### *11.1.4 Income Tax Continued to Grow, and the Industrial Industry Has Become the Main Taxpayer*

In 2017, ZLCs' income tax expenses totalled 56.3 billion yuan. Due to the increase in profitability of existing companies and the increase in income tax brought by newly listed companies, the total income tax increased by 41% y-o-y. The income tax expenses of ZLCs were continuously increasing, which represented both the improvement of their profitabilities and theirs economic and social contribution. At the same time, the Industrial industry replaced the Information Technology industry with its continuously growing profitability, and became the biggest income taxpayer. In 2017, its income tax expense reached 17.2 billion yuan (accounting for 31%). The structural changes of income tax expenses among different industries reflected the economic structure changes of ZLCs to some extent.

## 11.2 Problems Facing ZLCs

### *11.2.1 Financing Difficulties*

In 2017, with the reinforce of China's financial supervision and deleveraging, SMEs across the country were facing severe financing. ZLCs were no exception. In the same year, ZLCs explored diversified financing channels such as equity financing and debt financing, and reached a net financing amount of 226.3 billion yuan, down 8% y-o-y. In terms of direct finance, 25 newly listed ZLCs raised up 13.1 billion yuan in initial public offerings, down 6%. 29 ZLCs issued targeted stocks for 39 times, and raised up 39.8 billion yuan, a decline of 77% compared to the same period of the last year. 21 ZLCs issued 30 corporate bonds traded on exchanges and raised up 29.2 billion yuan, declining 74% y-o-y. It could be seen that in 2017, financing difficulties faced ZLCs. Both equity financing and debt financing were shrinking.

### *11.2.2 Stagnant Investment*

Expanding investment is the key to the innovation and development of companies. At present, regulatory policies on the usages of funds have been tighter; therefore, public companies were holding large amounts of cash that could not be used for investments. In 2017, the net investment of public ZLCs totaled 457.3 billion yuan, an increase of 12% (far lower than 104% in 2016). 132 ZLCs (42%) witnessed varied degrees of decline in net investment. Meanwhile, as of the end of 2017, ZLCs held cashes and the equivalents amounting to 874.6 billion yuan. As a result, ZLCs could not fully utilize their investment capabilities.

### *11.2.3 Stock Market Risks*

Listed companies are the main force of regional economy. Their risks in financial markets will affect the stability and coordinated development of security markets, society, and economy. Keeping security market risks under control will be of great significance for preventing systemic financial risks, maintaining the stability of financial systems, and promoting the development of economy. In terms of leverage ratio, in 2017, ZLCs' liabilities totaled 4039.0 billion yuan, up 11% y-o-y. The average asset-liability ratio was 63.32%. 61 ZLCs (19%) had a debt-to-asset ratio of over 60%. Some companies even had an asset-liability ratio of more than 100%. Under the background of "deleveraging" in recent years, the asset-liability ratio of ZLCs have not experienced an obvious decline. Some companies still had high leverage ratio and heavy burden on debt. Therefore, ZLCs still need to prevent potential risks.

## 11.3 Suggestions

### *11.3.1 Exploring Corporate Financing Channels and Meeting Funding Needs of Technology-Based Companies*

In 2017, ZLCs' net financing witnessed a decline compared to the same period of the previous year. Funds raised through channels of IPO, targeted stock issuance, bond issuance, and pledge of stock rights have seen varying degrees of decline. Deleveraging and shrinking financing channels made certain ZLCs strapped for cash and hard to achieve further developments. We suggest that innovative science companies should expand financing channels, multi-level capital market should be completed, and equity financing should be encouraged. Companies in trouble but with great technologies and management are encouraged to take market-oriented approaches such as restructuring debts or transferring debts into equities. Asset-light new economy enterprises should spend more on the innovation of financial products that take patents, intellectual property rights, and equities as pledges.

### *11.3.2 Promoting Investments and Investment Efficiency*

In 2017, ZLCs had cashes and equivalents of more than 874.6 billion yuan. The net outflow of cash flow from investment activities was 457.3 billion yuan. However, for some companies, the investment intensity and asset utilization still needed to be improved. Hence, it is recommended to encourage ZLCs to invest abroad on condition of obeying the relevant laws and regulations and following national industry-oriented strategies. Funds raised more than goal amount are supposed to be supervised when they are used for investment. Relaxing restrictions upon the use of funds by listed companies will effectively release the investment strength of ZLCs, for example, in key areas of energy conservation and environment protection, medical care, health care and education, which have long-term development potential and are related to national economy and people's livelihood, moderately lowering the threshold of cooperation shall be done and relevant listed companies shall be encouraged to participate in. All these can promote the long-term participation of social capital, and drive public company investments.

### *11.3.3 Strengthening Financial Risk Prevention and Improving the Liquidity of Business Capital*

For a high-quality development, national policies on financial regulation focuses on how to control financial risks, which is also the core for a company to pursue continuous economic development. It is recommended that ZLCs should properly arrange the liquidity and financing plans, and balance capital risks and efficiency. Relative government departments should serve companies in ways of helping companies raise their awareness of preventing financial risks, learning financial risks facing ZLCs timely, and helping companies properly avoid and cope with financial risks. In the meantime, it is recommended to improve capabilities of preventing and handling financial risks during the process of deleveraging, promoting the securitization of non-performing assets, and writing off and dealing with non-performing assets.

### *11.3.4 Strengthening Confidence and Boosting with Innovation*

China has been transferring its economy from high-speed growth to high-quality development. The market capitalization of ZLCs totaled around 5.5 trillion yuan, up 15%, a moderate growth. The total revenue was close to 4 trillion yuan, with an increase of 14% y-o-y. Net profit amount reached 167.8 billion yuan, an increase of 14% y-o-y. These data show that the current development of ZLCs is stable and powerful, and strategic emerging industries at Zhongguancun have been leading the development of capital markets in Beijing and even nationwide. It is recommended that ZLCs should work on technical innovation, and improve their technologies. It is believed that ZLCs will continuously support the establishment of national science and technology innovation center with its robust development and profit growth.

The manufacturer's authorised representative in the EU is Springer Nature Customer Service Centre GmbH, Europaplatz 3, 69115 Heidelberg, Germany. If you have any concerns regarding our products, please contact ProductSafety@springernature.com

Printed and bound by CPI Group (UK) Ltd, Croydon, CR0 4YY
30/09/2026
02225575-0013